RICKOVER

MILITARY PROFILES

SERIES EDITOR
Dennis E. Showalter, Ph.D.
Colorado College

Instructive summaries for general and expert readers alike, volumes in the Military Profiles series are essential treatments of significant and popular military figures drawn from world history, ancient times through the present.

RICKOVER

Father of the Nuclear Navy

Thomas B. Allen and Norman Polmar

Potomac Books, Inc.
Washington, D.C.

Library of Congress Cataloging-in-Publication Data
Allen, Thomas B.
   Rickover : father of the nuclear Navy / Thomas B. Allen and Norman Polmar.
    p. cm. — (Military profiles)
    Includes bibliographical references and index.
    1. Rickover, Hyman George. 2. United States. Navy—Officers—Biography. 3. Admirals—United States—Biography. 4. Nuclear submarines—United States—History. 5. Nuclear warships—United States—History. I. Polmar, Norman. II. Title.

V63.R54A55 2007
359.0092—dc22
[B]

                                    2006023386

Hardcover ISBN-13: 978-1-57488-445-6
Softcover ISBN-13: 978-1-57488-704-4 (alk. paper)

Printed in the United States of America on acid-free paper that meets the American National Standards Institute Z39-48 Standard.

Potomac Books, Inc.
22841 Quicksilver Drive
Dulles, Virginia 20166

First Edition

10 9 8 7 6 5 4 3 2 1

*To our friends who went down to the sea
in Admiral Rickover's submarines*

Contents

Admiral Hyman George Rickover was a remarkable man. Almost singlehandly and against major opposition from within the Navy—according to legend—he built a "nuclear navy" of submarines, cruisers, and giant aircraft carriers, all propelled by the atom.

Like most legends, there is some truth to the accounts of how Rickover built the Nuclear Navy. He did face opposition, and he did overcome it, often breaking the rules or—thanks to his unique position of being "double hatted" within the Navy and the Atomic Energy Commission— making up his own. In doing so, he certainly overcame the bureaucratic inertia, government regulations, and contracting policies that delayed his drive for a nuclear navy.

However, one can find no opposition to the development of nuclear-propelled submarines per se in the U.S. Navy, and there is no evidence that—except on the basis of cost—the Navy, in the person of decision-making offices, preferred non-nuclear ships to those with nuclear propulsion. Indeed, the U.S. Navy had officially shown an interest in nuclear propulsion as early as 1939, and after World War II initiated a nuclear submarine program before Rickover became involved.

As one admiral put it, Rickover was not "the father of the nuclear submarine," but he was the expediter of its components, and his ill-tempered nature was necessary to make it happen. He was the driving force for development of the first nuclear submarine, the USS *Nautilus*. He was able to bring about that great accomplishment because his superiors in the Navy Department had actively supported the building of the submarine, and because his superior in the Bureau of Ships had placed him in position to accomplish it.

More submarines followed the *Nautilus*, and then came nuclear-propelled surface warships. Three and a half years after the *Nautilus* went to sea, the Soviet Union sent its first nuclear submarine to sea. But that Soviet submarine, the *K-3*, later named *Leninsky Komsomol* (for the youth group honoring V. I. Lenin), was faster, deeper-diving, and quieter than the *Nautilus*.

Officially, Rickover was responsible only for the propulsion plant for nuclear submarines, but he continually increased his role in the design and development of the total ship, especially after the tragic loss of the nuclear-propelled submarine *Thresher* in 1963. In addition, Rickover personally selected and trained the commanding officers of most U.S. nuclear submarines up to 1981, and he developed the training program for nuclear officers. This was done primarily under his "hat" as head of nuclear ship programs for the Atomic Energy Commission (later the Department of Energy).

Rickover's selection of officers and senior enlisted men for nuclear training—from the best and the brightest candidates available—generally provided outstanding commanding officers and other personnel for U.S. nuclear submarines, and subsequently, for the engineering departments of nuclear surface ships. Officers and enlisted men in the nuclear program were well-trained, far better than their Soviet counterparts, and they were a major factor in the relatively safe record of U.S. nuclear submarines and surface ships. Also, Rickover-trained personnel have been the core of the U.S. civilian nuclear power industry.

The cost of his control, however, was high. Many good men were thrown by the wayside in Rickover's selection process. Civilians and officers who questioned Rickover's practices or policies often had their careers ruined. Additionally, Rickover's control of personnel assignments produced many problems for the Navy. During the Cold War, there were continually critical shortfalls in submarine officer retention, especially after the early 1960s. This was when the Navy developed—with little input from Rickover—the Polaris missile system, and in a brief period built forty-one submarines to carry that weapon, each manned by two crews.

Still, it was Rickover who provided the drive, the standards of excellence, and the strategy for building the nuclear navy.

Many individuals and organizations assisted us in writing our major biography, *Admiral Rickover: Controversy and Genius* (1982). We have used much of the research for that volume for this project.

We are very appreciative of Rick Russell of Potomac Books for asking us to produce this book, and of Ms. Michie Shaw for the book's production.

Thomas B. Allen and Norman Polmar

1898, August 24	Rickover born in Makow, Poland (according to school records).
1900, January 27	Rickover born in Makow, Poland (according to Navy records).
1904	Comes to America with mother and sister Fanny.
1918, February	Graduates from John Marshall High School (Chicago) with honors.
1918, June 29	Enters the Naval Academy.
1922, June 2	Graduates from the Naval Academy and commissioned as ensign.
1922, August 13	Reports for duty aboard destroyer *Percival* at San Diego.
1922, September 5	Reports for duty aboard destroyer *La Vallette* at San Francisco.
1923, June 21	Becomes engineering officer of *La Vallette*.
1925, January 21	Reports for duty aboard battleship *Nevada* at Bremerton, Washington.
1925, May 20	Transferred to hospital ship *Relief* for treatment.
1925, June	Promoted to lieutenant (junior grade).
1925, September	Returns to *Nevada*; made electrical officer.
1927, April 28	Departs *Nevada* at Hampton Roads, Virginia.
1927, June	Reports to Naval Postgraduate School in Annapolis.

1928, June	Promoted to lieutenant.
1928–1929	Attends Columbia University; earns MS in electrical engineering.
1929, October 10	Reports to submarine *S-9* at New London, Connecticut.
1930, January–June	Attends Submarine School at New London.
1930, June 21	Reports for duty to submarine *S-48* at New London.
1931, March 1	*S-48* arrives at Coco Solo, Canal Zone.
1931, June	Becomes executive officer of *S-48*.
1931, August 4	Qualifies for submarine command.
1931, October 8	Marries Ruth Dorothy Masters in Litchfield, Connecticut.
1933, June 5	Detached from *S-48*.
1933, July 5	Reports as Inspector of Naval Material, Philadelphia.
1935, April 13	Reports for duty to battleship *New Mexico* at Los Angeles as assistant engineering officer.
1937, June	Detached from *New Mexico*.
1937, July 1	Promoted to lieutenant commander.
1937, July 17	Becomes commanding officer of minesweeper *Finch* at Tsingtao, China.
1937, October 5	Relieved as commanding officer of *Finch*. Departs ship October 24.
1937, November 1	Arrives for duty at Cavite Navy Yard in the Philippines.
1938	The Rickovers tour Southeast Asia.
1939, March	Naval Research Laboratory, Washington, D.C., initiates research about nuclear ship propulsion.
1939, August	Reports to Bureau of Engineering (soon to become Bureau of Ships) in Washington. Albert Einstein

	signs a letter to President Roosevelt advising of the potential of atomic energy for weapons.
1940, October 11	Son, Robert Masters, born.
1942, January 1	Promoted to commander.
1942, June	Promoted to captain (temporary).
1945	Heads special study team at Naval Supply Center in Mechanicsburg, Pennsylvania.
1945, July	Becomes commander of ship repair facility on Okinawa.
1945, December	Becomes inspector general of 19th Fleet in San Francisco, supervising mothballing of warships.
1946, March	Dr. Philip Abelson completes Navy study "Atomic Energy Submarine."
1946, May	Assigned to Manhattan Project at Oak Ridge, Tennessee.
1946, June	Arrives at Oak Ridge.
1947, January 9	Adm. Chester W. Nimitz, Chief of Naval Operations, approves nuclear submarine development program.
1947, August 19	Dr. Edward Teller formally supports Rickover and a nuclear propulsion program.
1947, September	Assigned to BuShips staff of Adm. Earle Mills.
1947, December 5	Adm. Nimitz formally recommends nuclear propulsion program to the Secretary of the Navy.
1948, August 4	Adm. Mills establishes Nuclear Power Branch in BuShips under Rickover.
1949, February	Additionally appointed to Division of Reactor Development in the Atomic Energy Commission.
1950, January	Begins discussions of construction of a nuclear submarine with Electric Boat Company.
1951, July	Passed over by Navy board for selection to rear admiral.

1951, August 20	First nuclear submarine ordered from Electric Boat Company.
1952, June 14	President Truman presides at keel laying for *Nautilus*.
1952, June	Passed over by flag selection board for second time. Must retire by mid-1953.
1953, March 30	*Nautilus* reactor prototype goes critical at Arco, Idaho.
1953, July 1	Selected for promotion to rear admiral by special board.
1953, October	Placed in charge of power reactor program at Shippingport, Pennsylvania.
1954, January 11	*Time* cover story on Rickover.
1954, January 21	Mrs. Eisenhower christens the *Nautilus*.
1955, January 15	*Nautilus* gets underway for first time.
1958, August 3	*Nautilus* reaches the North Pole.
1958, October 24	Promoted to vice admiral.
1959, July	Accompanies Vice President Nixon to Soviet Union; visits nuclear icebreaker *Lenin* at Leningrad shipyard.
1962, January 27	Reaches statutory age for retirement from Navy; extended on active duty.
1972, May 25	Wife, Ruth Masters, dies.
1973, December 3	Promoted to admiral.
1974, January 19	Marries Eleonore Ann Bednowicz.
1981, January	Retired from active duty.
1986, July 8	Adm. Rickover dies.

RICKOVER

Victory at Sea

Worrld War II—the most devastating and costly conflict in history—came to an end on September 2, 1945, when Japanese and Allied representatives signed the surrender accord on the deck of the U.S. battleship *Missouri*. At anchor in Tokyo Bay around the dreadnought were hundreds of U.S. warships, and when the brief ceremony was concluded, almost 1,000 U.S. carrier-based aircraft and 462 B-29 Superfortress heavy bombers flew over the *Missouri*. The U.S. Navy's aerial armada came from the massive carrier task force operating off the Japanese coast, which was kept at sea just in case the Japanese surrender was some kind of ghastly deception.

The U.S. naval forces that were present in the Western Pacific were but a part of the massive fleet that the United States had put to sea for the war against Japan and Germany. The U.S. Navy had more surface ships than the combined totals of all of the Allied and enemy navies. In every theater, those ships, along with submarines and aircraft, played key roles in Allied victories.

The Navy's Bureau of Ships was responsible for building and maintaining those ships, including the electrical systems that were vital for all of the surface ships and submarines. Propulsion in some ships and all of the submarines, fire control systems, many weapons, air conditioning, radar, radios, sonar, signal lights, interior lighting, and even stoves and refrigerators all depended upon electricity and electric motors. The officer who directed the Electrical Section of the Bureau of Ships—called BuShips in Navy jargon—and who was responsible for those electrical systems was Captain Hyman George Rickover.

Rickover came to BuShips in August 1939. Less than two years earlier, Rickover had become an engineering duty officer, a specialist who would spend the rest of his career in BuShips, at shipyards, or at naval bases, working on the designing, building, repairing, and maintaining of Navy ships. At BuShips, Rickover learned how to deal with bureaucracies, and how to leverage his important position into dictating terms and conditions to the industrial firms that were providing electrical equipment to the Navy. Rickover was both dedicated and competent. He worked hard and demanded the same of his subordinates in BuShips— both military and civilian—and from his contractors.

He did an excellent job as head of the Electrical Section; however, like all naval officers, he wanted an assignment in a combat theater. For an engineering duty officer, such an assignment would be on a fleet staff or at a forward base. After several appeals for such duty by Rickover, his immediate superior, Rear Admiral Earle W. Mills, Deputy Chief of BuShips, assigned him briefly to conduct a study at the naval supply center in Mechanicsburg, Pennsylvania. Then, Rickover received orders to command a repair facility at Baten Ko on the Pacific island of Okinawa, which had been recently captured from the Japanese after savage fighting.

The Okinawa facility would be vital for the forthcoming U.S. invasion of Japan, the first phase of which was planned for November 1945. Those landings would have constituted the largest invasion in history, exceeding the D-Day landings in Normandy. The landings on Kyushu, the southernmost of Japan's main islands, were to be made by nine divisions—six Army and three Marine—with several follow-up divisions coming ashore as needed. Many hundreds of U.S. warships and hundreds more amphibious and landing ships and craft were to participate in the assault. The Japanese defensive strategy called for the American invasion to be slowed or turned back by inflicting tens of thousands of casualties on the invading troops. The Kyushu defenses would include ruthless attacks on the ships and landing craft by suicide (kamikaze) aircraft, small craft laden with explosives, midget submarines, manned torpedoes, and even swimmers who would attempt to place explosives under the hulls of landing craft. American casualties, the Japanese hoped, would force negotiations to end the fighting.

Those U.S. ships and craft that were damaged in the landings were to make their way back to, or be towed to, the repair facility on Okinawa, some 350 miles from Kyushu. There, Rickover's repair facility would undertake to mend and restore the ships and craft so that they could be used for follow-up operations against Kyushu, and then in the landings planned for the main island of Honshu in the spring of 1946.

The atomic bombs that brought an end to the war in August 1945 made obsolete not only the plans that had centered on Okinawa, but also the men working there. There was no need to do much more than close down the facility and move out, abandoning much of the equipment, which would not be needed in peacetime. But Rickover insisted that whatever could be salvaged from his base had to be packed up and shipped back to the United States. It was not much of a base—tents, some metal Quonset huts, and other temporary buildings—but it was Rickover's command.

Then, on October 9, 1945, Typhoon Louise whipped along the eastern edge of Okinawa, killing at least thirty-six persons and destroying nearly everything in its path. The piers at the main naval base disappeared. Nine small ships were sunk and more than 175 other craft were carried ashore on mountainous waves to be left high and dry.

Many of the smaller bases were devastated. Some 60 to 80 percent of the tents and buildings on the island were damaged or destroyed. The worst hit was Rickover's facility. The official damage estimate put the amount of destruction to his repair facility at 99 percent. The following day, he began supervising the cleanup and the repair. But only Rickover could have believed that the U.S. Navy still needed a ship-repair base on Okinawa two months after the war had ended.

Rickover, with nothing to command, lingered on Okinawa until November 26. Two days later, his naval repair base, which no longer existed, was officially declared inactivated and expunged from the record. For Rickover, World War II had ended in ruins at a quiet cove on Okinawa.

In 1945, he had twenty-three years of active naval service and held the temporary rank of captain. He was eligible for retirement, if he wished. The need for engineering duty officers in the postwar Navy was limited. No new ships would be designed for at least several years, and after those hulls still on the building ways were completed (or, in many cases, scrapped without being completed), there would be few if any new ships built. The perception of lasting peace made it unlikely that there would be a large postwar fleet. And, as the *Enola Gay*'s atomic bomb had so dramatically demonstrated, if there were to be a conflict, the long-range bomber carrying an atomic bomb would be the immediate and final arbitrator of it.

What, then, could be the future of the U.S. Navy—and of temporary Captain Rickover?

2

Father's Occupation: Tailor

Hyman George Rickover was born into a medieval world, a Europe of emperor and peasant, a land of poverty, a place of fear. The empire was Russian, ruled by a tsar. The land was Poland, a conquered province within the empire. His place of birth was the Jewish Pale.

He was one of about five million Jews of the Pale, where Polish Jews could not own land and were barred from most education. The Jews lived in terror of the pogroms that came unexpectedly upon villages like a summer storm. Rickover's father, born Eliachako but known as Abraham, had seen as a child an outburst of anti-Jewish pogroms in 1881 and 1882.

Abraham Rickover made a living as a tailor in Makow. He had married and was beginning to raise a family when the lure of America reached the Polish provinces of the Pale. Abraham arrived in New York sometime around 1904, and after two years of hard work he had saved enough to send for his family—Ruchal, Fanny, and Hyman, who was about six.[1] "My sister and I ran around the lower decks while my mother sat on the steel deck the entire time, guarding the sheet with all our worldly possessions,"

Rickover once recounted. "The second-class passengers from the deck above occasionally threw us children an apple or orange, as we looked up at them from between decks."

Abraham Rickover worked as a tailor in New York as well.[2] He had invested in an apartment building in Brooklyn and had expected his family to settle there, but he lost his investment in the depression of 1907. A year later, soon after the birth of Hitel (her American name would be Augusta), the Rickover family headed for Chicago, the city that Hyman Rickover would always consider his hometown.

Hyman entered Chicago's John Marshall High School in September 1914. One record indicates his birth date as June 1898. Another gives August 24, 1898. He graduated as a member of the February class of 1918. Rickover became a Western Union messenger while in high school, and one of his most frequent calls was to the Chicago office of Representative Adolph Joachim Sabath, a Democrat. He had been elected to Congress for the first time in 1906 and would make a record by remaining there continuously until his death in 1952.

The heart of Sabath's district was the Jewish immigrant neighborhood in which the Rickovers lived. Rickover was introduced to Sabath as a fellow Jewish immigrant; thus was initiated a relationship that was first highlighted by Rickover's appointment to the U.S. Navy Academy by Sabath, and that would continue for decades. Sabath's successor in the position, informally known as "the Jewish Congressman," was Sidney R. Yates. Yates would help to make Captain Rickover an admiral, and he would help Admiral Rickover build a nuclear navy.

Each Representative and Senator was allowed to nominate five young men for admission to the Navy Academy in 1918, but Rickover still had to pass the entrance examinations. He briefly attended a prep school, but unsatisfied with its approach to readying young men for the examinations, he isolated himself in his boarding house for two months and studied intensely on his own.

He passed the examinations and was admitted to the Naval Academy for the class of 1922. Each plebe signed himself in, writing in a ledger that asked religious affiliation (Rickover wrote "Hebrew") and father's occupation (Rickover wrote "tailor"). In the summer of 1918, the Great War was ending and, by the time the Armistice came in November 1918, the Naval Academy became less a place where a man studied war and more a place where young men prepared for an exciting, romantic, and socially acceptable career. The Academy was, for some, as much a part of the Ivy League as Yale or Harvard. The young men belonged to fraternities, took debutantes to dances (or, in the Academy slang, "dragged Four-O debs to hops"), and stuck together. They called themselves "Our Set" and "Blood." And many of the blood were truly that, for they were the sons and grandsons of naval officers.

The more typical midshipmen were young men of farms and small towns, along with one hundred enlisted men from the Navy and Marine Corps who entered Annapolis from the fleet. All—the blood, the sons of Navy, the sailors, the Marines, the ordinary, and the undistinguished—lived in what appeared officially to be a classless society. But men of similar origins tended to stick together and they roomed together in Bancroft Hall.

Bancroft Hall was the largest dormitory in the world. The huge building was designed to house all midshipmen, with four plebes or two upperclassmen to a room. But not even Bancroft Hall, with its rooms for 2,200, could accommodate the entire regiment of midshipmen, which was growing toward 2,250 during the war. Most of the rooms were occupied by upperclassmen when the first of 898 plebes began coming through the gates in Annapolis in the summer of 1918. Those in the first wave got rooms in Bancroft Hall. Latecomers were put up at the old Marine Barracks on the northern end of the Academy grounds. One of the latecomers was Rickover, who spent his first weeks at Annapolis in the hospital—he was diagnosed with diphtheria, often fatal at that time.

What would become his lifelong dislike for Annapolis and its ways began in the Marine Barracks, where he bunked alone in semi-isolation during his recovery. His resentment could still be discerned decades later in his description of his days at Annapolis.

Looking back, he remembered how his late-night studying "irritated the other midshipmen." Too poor to have much of a social life, Rickover spent most of his time in his room with his books.

At the top of the Class of 1922 there was a fierce competition for Number One. Rickover was not a contender, but later in his career it would be incorrectly recalled, once even by a Chief of Naval Operations, that Rickover had been fighting to head his class. The duel was actually between Jerauld L. Olmsted and Leonard Kaplan. Olmsted was one of the most popular members of the class; Kaplan's classmates—egged on by Olmsted—had condemned him to live alone in an obscure corner of Bancroft Hall. Kaplan, in the saying of the day, had been "sent to Coventry": During all of his four years at the Naval Academy, no midshipmen could speak to him; no one could acknowledge his existence.

What happened to Leonard Kaplan at Annapolis would, through the years, become intertwined with what happened to Rickover at Annapolis. Kaplan's real ordeal would be eclipsed by tales of Rickover, in which his name was substituted for Kaplan's. Navy people knew that hazing was unbridled in those days, and they knew that Rickover, as a "grind"—someone who puts books ahead of girls—was a natural target of hazing. They also knew that Jews were often targets. So, many years after Annapolis, when Rickover was fighting to be promoted to admiral, the Kaplan stories circulated as Rickover stories. In the social climate of Annapolis of the 1920s, the hazing of a Jew would seem to be inevitable, as would the failure of a Jew to become an admiral in the 1950s.

Although Rickover, like Kaplan, was a grind and shunned extracurricular activities, he could not attain the excellence that Kaplan achieved. Rickover graduated 106th in a class of 539. Kaplan's chief competitor, Olmsted, had entered Annapolis from the ranks of enlisted men. In his graduation year he was regimental commander and editor in chief of the yearbook, *The Lucky Bag*. Each biographical page of *The Lucky Bag* contained two large photographs of graduating midshipmen. Under each photograph was a short commentary that usually dwelt on the subject's physique, ancestry, or dating and study habits. ("Rickie," says Rickover's biography, was "rarely seen" with a date; but the comments about him were positive.)

Kaplan's photo and biography appear on a page that is perforated, so that it could be easily and cleanly torn from the yearbook. The perforated page was Olmsted's idea; he graduated as Number One to Kaplan's Number Two. In later years, many officers would claim that the perforated page had been the one with Rickover's photo.

------◆◆◆◆------

Of the 539 graduates of the Class of 1922, only 390 were commissioned as ensigns in the Navy, and 24 as second lieutenants in the Marine Corps. Most new ensigns were assigned to battleships, and Rickover was assigned to the destroyer *La Vallette*, based at San Diego.

Rickover spent most of his off-duty hours curled up with a book or crawling through the ship's engineering spaces, studying the steam plant as she sailed south to join several other warships off the western coasts of Mexico and Central America. His interest in *La Vallette*'s cramped, hot, noisy engineering spaces led to his being named engineering officer of the ship. His responsibilities included maintenance and operation of the ship's massive steam-propulsion plant and its numerous auxiliary components.

His next assignment, in January 1925, took him to Bremerton, Washington, where he boarded the new battleship *Nevada.* He had barely settled in when the Battle Fleet departed for Hawaii, the Navy's forward exercise area in the Pacific. There, the U.S. Fleet prepared for a goodwill cruise to Australia and New Zealand. Rickover, on sick leave, did not make the cruise, but he was promoted to lieutenant (junior grade) and returned to the *Nevada* in early September, reporting on board as the battleship's electrical officer. Rickover learned everything that could be found out about his equipment. He made time for little else, except reading.

After five years of sea duty, Rickover was sent to postgraduate school—a year's course in electrical engineering at the Naval Academy in Annapolis, and, as a "full" lieutenant, to study for an advanced degree at Columbia University in New York. There, in June 1928, he met Ruth Masters, who was doing graduate work in international law. A native of Washington, D.C., she had lived abroad for several years and was at Columbia on a scholarship.

Rickover's shore life ended in 1929 when, after receiving orders to report to the battleship *California* as electrical officer, he volunteered for submarine duty. The submarine branch of the Navy was small: the crews of all sixty-nine Navy submarines at the time totaled slightly more than the crew of two battleships. Submarines were small, cramped, dirty from diesel oil, and they smelled. There was a standing joke about being able to tell a submarine sailor in the dark because of the stench of diesel oil that permeated his skin and clothes. That, however, was no joke. To Rickover, the submarine branch offered an engineering challenge, especially with his new knowledge of electrical engineering. All submarines were propelled underwater by electric motors, with energy provided by storage batteries. (When the submarines were on the surface, they were propelled by diesel engines, which also charged the storage batteries.)

Rickover reported to the submarine base at New London, Connecticut. On October 10, 1929, he went aboard the submarine *S-9* for temporary duty, to await the start of the next submarine-training course, which began in January 1930. In his spare time he played little, but read, studied, and corresponded with Ruth Masters, then in Paris.

After completing a six-month course at New London, Rickover was assigned as engineer and electrical officer of the submarine *S-48*, which would have a four-year stay in the area of the Panama Canal as part of a protective force. In mid-1931, Rickover was promoted to executive officer and navigator—the senior officer on board after the commanding officer. A short time later he completed the training requirements to qualify for submarine command. That meant that when his tour as "exec" of the *S-48* was completed, the Bureau of Navigation would likely assign him to command of a submarine.[3]

In the fall of 1931, Rickover took leave and returned to the United States. His correspondence courtship of Ruth Masters ended successfully on October 8, when they were married in Litchfield, Connecticut, by an Episcopal priest. During the four years since Ruth Masters and Rickover had first met at Columbia, she had studied at the Sorbonne in Paris and begun her studies for a doctorate in international relations. Her book, *International Law in National Court,* would be published in 1932. At this time, Rickover advised his parents that he no longer considered himself a Jew.

In June 1931, Rickover was relieved as executive officer of the *S-48.* He received no orders to command a submarine. Instead, a month later, he was assigned to the Office of the Inspector of Naval Material in Philadelphia for two years of shore duty. His next assignment took him to sea as the assistant engineering officer of the battleship *New Mexico.* While he was on the *New Mexico*, the ship won three annual engineering "E" awards for efficiency in succession, thanks to such power-saving Rickover innovations as shortening the showers for junior officers.

Rickover was a lieutenant commander when he left the battleship and was assigned to command of the USS *Finch,* a rundown, 188-foot wooden minesweeper, built in 1918 for service in the North Sea. When Rickover took command, the *Finch* was towing targets and carrying supplies on Chinese waters. Japan had invaded China and war raged around the *Finch*, but the ship was usually motionless, and so, it appeared, was Rickover's naval career. He held command—his first and only—for just three months. The official correspondence and reports concerning his relief after so short a time have been lost, but contemporaries told the authors of this book that he was "relieved for cause."

Rickover then made a drastic change of course, asking to be designated as an Engineering Duty Officer (EDO). As an EDO, he would be, for the remainder of his naval career, a specialist in ship design, construction, and repair. In that role he could not expect to go to sea, except possibly on a commodore's or admiral's staff. He would normally serve ashore at Navy headquarters or at navy yards or other facilities.

Rickover's decision was fateful, for not only would it chart the path of his career, it would also be the reason for much of the controversy and confusion decades later when Congress challenged the Navy's decision not to promote Rickover to rear admiral. Relatively few people outside of the Navy realized that by law and tradition the Navy differentiated between line officers, who could command ships (*line* traced back to "ships of the line"), and engineering officers, who could design, operate, and maintain ships. An engineering officer wore the star insignia of a line officer, but the EDO designation would make him a "restricted" line officer, the principal restriction being that he could not command ships or operating forces.

When Rickover made his decision, there were only three EDO rear admirals in the Navy. All three were inspectors of machinery at major industrial concerns doing work for the Navy. No higher EDO rank was possible at the time. For Rickover to advance would be difficult, because most engineering duty officers had become engineering specialists earlier in their careers. But Rickover believed that his postgraduate education, his engineering experience at sea, and his intensive study of machinery would more than compensate for his late entry into the EDO ranks.

He was ordered first to the Cavite Navy Yard in the Philippines as assistant planning officer. After two years there, he was ordered to the Bureau of Engineering in Washington, the home of the Navy's EDOs.

Initially, Rickover was assigned to the Design Division of the Bureau of Engineering (which became the Bureau of Ships on June 20, 1942). Some of the Navy's best brains devoted to ship and submarine design were concentrated in that division, including Commander Earle W. Mills, a veteran naval engineer who would have a major impact on Rickover's career. Indeed, much of Rickover's ability to survive and his success both in BuShips and the early Navy nuclear-propulsion program would be due to Mills. And it would be here, in BuShips, where Rickover would first learn bureaucratic warfare. He was in a power center, for to a great extent the Navy's technical bureaus ruled the Navy.

As head of the Electrical Section during World War II, Rickover worked day and night, including weekends, and he drove his staff just as hard. He traveled frequently, nagging contractors and visiting shipyards where war-damaged ships were being repaired. "He liked to travel on Sundays," a staffer remembered, "and he always carried the pinks," referring to a practice Rickover originated.

The pinks were carbon copies of all correspondence, including memos and informal notes. Every secretary was instructed to give to Rickover at the end of each working day copies of all correspondence that had passed through her typewriter. Rickover read every word of every pink, and if he spotted a grammatical error or something else he did not like, he would call in the author and dress him down, sometimes punctuating the lecture by grinding the offending pink under his heel or balling it and tossing it in the general direction of the waste-paper basket. Later, even in the age of Xerox, Rickover would retain the "pinks system" that he invented in the Electrical Section.

On his trips he wore civilian clothes whenever possible, and this too would become a habit. So would his insistence on saving government money by staying in a contractor's or colleague's home instead of a hotel, or by staying in the cheapest room in a hotel.

Those who knew Rickover then agreed that he was not trying to be exasperating. He had seen, from his vantage point in the Electrical Section, a Navy that had gone into war ill-managed and ill-prepared. He had seen electrical equipment put out of commission not only by the shocks of combat but also by mere moisture. He had seen how minor damage to a bulkhead could cripple a ship because behind the bulkhead lay unprotected cable and, when that was severed, fire-control systems or vital pumps were knocked out. He had learned that a system called battle lighting failed in battle. The system was not designed to hold up under sustained combat; the bulbs were blue, and sailors going on watch had trouble adjusting from darkness to blue light. Rickover succeeded in getting the lights changed from blue to red. But he had to fight to get this done, and to him it seemed as if he had to fight to get *anything* done. Rickover became angry at the Navy, and it would be an anger that would never cease.

3

The Navy and the Atom

At the beginning of the twentieth century, most submarines had primitive and dangerous gasoline engines to propel them on the surface and to recharge storage batteries that provided energy to their electric motors for underwater propulsion. Beginning in 1912, diesel engines provided a more efficient and reliable surface propulsion. Underwater speeds were low, a maximum of ten knots or less, with battery power to propel them for a few minutes at that speed, or for several hours or even a day at "creeping" speeds.

Because gasoline and the later diesel engines required oxygen for combustion, in order to recharge their batteries the submarines had to come to the surface, where they were vulnerable to detection. And because of the limitations of a battery charge, the submarines had to come to the surface at frequent intervals. This situation was partially mitigated by the German submarine force in World War II when, using a Dutch invention, the Germans fitted snorkel (*schnorchel*) breathing tubes to their submarines to permit air to be brought in for the diesel engines while the submarine was operating just beneath the surface.[4] Although this made the submarines more difficult to detect visually, radar could detect the snorkel masts protruding above the water, and soon development was underway on "sniffers" that could also detect the snorkel's diesel exhaust fumes.

During World War II, German scientists and engineers initiated two types of highly advanced submarines that went to sea at the end of the war as the Type XXI and Type XVII U-boats. The Type XXI U-boat, or *unterseebot,* had a streamlined hull devoid of protuberances such as chocks, cleats, or large guns. Instead of a large conning tower with gun platforms and an internal pressure chamber that served as an attack center, the Type XXI had a streamlined sail, or fairwater, around the shears that supported the periscopes and other masts and antennas. These features reduced the drag above the waterline to about one sixth that of earlier submarines.

There were also improvements in the submarine's torpedo reload system, crew living conditions, and operating depth. But the most impressive feature of the Type XXI was its underwater speed:

16 knots for 25 nautical miles
12 knots for 60 nautical miles
6 knots for 280 nautical miles

Thus, the Type XXI U-boat was more than half again as fast underwater as contemporary U.S. submarines, and could maintain that top speed for one and a half hours, compared to the few minutes that a U.S. submarine could run at ten knots. This performance was achieved by a large increase in the number of batteries in the submarine and an increase in the voltage to the main electric motors.[5]

Even greater underwater performance was promised for the Type XVII U-boat, the "ultimate" submarine envisioned by German officials during the war. This was a closed-cycle or single-drive submarine that would employ an air-independent propulsion system to drive the submarine on both the surface and underwater, the latter at speeds of some twenty-five knots or more.

The principal closed-cycle propulsion system was developed in the 1930s by Helmuth Walter and was based on the decomposition of highly concentrated hydrogen peroxide, or perhydrol. In the submarine the perhydrol was brought in contact with the catalyst necessary to cause decomposition in a complex system. This produced steam and oxygen at a high temperature—1,765°F (963°C)—which then passed into a combustion chamber where they combined to ignite diesel oil, while water was sprayed on the gas to increase its volume and decrease its temperature. The combination steam-gas was then used to drive a turbine.

The year 1940 saw the highly successful trials of the first Walter-propulsion submarine, the experimental *V-80*, which briefly reached a speed of twenty-six knots. The *V-80* was followed by an order for four Type XVIIA development submarines. Completed in 1943–44, these U-boats achieved speeds up to twenty-five knots submerged. But the Walter boats were plagued by mechanical and maintenance problems. Also, efficiency was low and significant power was lost because of the increase in back pressure on the exhaust system as the submarine went deeper. Still, construction of operational Walter boats—the Types XVIIB, XVIII, and later XXVIW—was initiated. The last were expected to achieve twenty-four knots submerged with an endurance of almost 160 nautical miles at that speed.

However, U.S. and British strategic bombing of Germany, numerous design changes, faulty construction procedures, and other factors delayed the production of the Type XXI and Walter submarine programs until they arrived too late to influence the conflict. Although hundreds of U-boats were ordered, with both propulsion systems, only a single Type XXI U-boat undertook an operational patrol before Germany surrendered in May 1945. (The smaller Type XXIII U-boats, similar in design to the Type XXI, became operational in February 1945. Five of these three-hundred-ton, twelve-knot submarines went to sea, carrying out eight short-duration patrols against Allied merchant shipping from late January 1945. These electro-boats sank six Allied ships without a loss.)

After the war, U.S., British, and Soviet engineers and naval officers picked through the ruins of the U-boat factories and ship-yards. They evaluated German submarine designs and propulsion systems, and many U-boat features were incorporated into the submarines of the Allied navies. Although underwater performance was improved, there were still the limitations of the need for periodic operation of the diesel engines (requiring oxygen) and the amount of perhydrol that could be carried—the latter involving a complex and, at times, dangerous process.

❦

Even before World War II began in Europe in September 1939, the U.S. Navy expressed interest in another form of submarine propulsion: atomic energy. In 1938, German scientists Otto Hahn and Fritz Strassmann had determined that a few atoms would split when uranium atoms were bombarded with neutrons, thereby releasing tremendous amounts of energy. This process of splitting atoms is called fission. The announcement of their findings created great excitement in scientific circles, including physicists at the U.S. Naval Research Laboratory in southeast Washington, D.C.

One of the nation's leading physicists, Dr. George Pegram of Columbia University, proposed a meeting early in 1939 with Navy researchers to discuss the practical uses of uranium fission. According to Dr. Ross Gunn of the Naval Research Laboratory, "it was recognized immediately that perhaps here was an answer to submarine propulsion problems." On March 17, 1939, Pegram met with Gunn; Rear Admiral Harold Bowen, Chief of the Bureau of Steam Engineering; Captain Hollis Cooley, head of the laboratory; and Dr. Enrico Fermi, the world's leading authority on the properties of neutrons. Fermi expressed the view that if certain problems relative to chemical purity were solved, the chances were good that a nuclear chain reaction could be initiated to make a super-explosive bomb through the use of uranium fission.

Dr. Gunn recalled that "hearing these outstanding scientists support the theory of a nuclear chain reaction gave us the guts necessary to present our plans for nuclear propulsion to the Navy." On March 20, Gunn and Cooley called on Admiral Bowen to outline a plan for a "fission chamber" that would generate steam to operate a turbine for a submarine propulsion plant. Gunn told the admiral that he had never thought he would seriously propose such a fantastic program to a responsible Navy official, but here was just such a proposal. He said that $1,500 was needed for initial research into the phenomenon of nuclear fission.

Admiral Bowen, an innovator who had fought many senior naval officers to get them to adopt steam turbines in place of reciprocating engines for surface ships, approved the funds. The $1,500 was the first money spent by the U.S. government for the study of nuclear fission. That summer, Gunn submitted his first report on nuclear propulsion for submarines. His report was four months ahead of the famous letter signed by Albert Einstein urging President Franklin D. Roosevelt to have the United States undertake a nuclear weapons program.

The war in Europe, American participation in the Atlantic battle against U-boats in the form of the Neutrality Patrol, and rapid U.S. rearmament all combined to overshadow the Navy's small nuclear effort. The 1942 establishment of the Manhattan Project to develop an atomic bomb halted the Navy's efforts completely, with Dr. Gunn and others becoming involved in research to support the project.

In 1944, Major General Leslie Groves, the head of the Manhattan Project, appointed a four-man committee to look into potential postwar uses of atomic energy. Two of the committee members were naval officers, one being Rear Admiral Earle W. Mills, who, as Assistant Chief of the Bureau of Ships, was the boss of then-Captain Rickover. The other two members were civilians. The committee, which was named for its chairman, Dr. Richard C. Tolman, the longtime dean of the California Institute of Technology's graduate school, visited the Naval Research Laboratory in the fall of 1944, where they were urged to give a nuclear-propelled submarine high priority in their report. In its formal report in December, the committee proposed that "the government should initiate and push, as an urgent project, research and development studies to provide power from nuclear sources for the propulsion of naval vessels."

Following the Allied victory over Germany and Japan in 1945 and a reevaluation of American progress in atomic energy, several scientists and engineers were discussing the possibility of nuclear submarines. Gunn and Philip H. Abelson of the Carnegie Institution, who in 1939 had worked on separating the lighter U235 atoms from the heavier uranium atoms for the Naval Research Laboratory, turned their attention back to the issue of an atomic submarine. Abelson took an advanced German U-boat design and developed a scheme for a nuclear "pile"—the term for a power-producing reactor—that could fit into existing spaces with only minor submarine design changes. Abelson's report had many shortcomings. For example, there was little information about the design of the nuclear pile. Still, his report "Atomic Energy Submarine," captured the imagination of many naval officers. The report stated that "only about two years would be required to put into operation an atomic-powered submarine mechanically capable of operation at 26 knots to 30 knots submerged for many years without surfacing or refueling."

The report had two "ifs" about the possibility of meeting the two-year timetable: The Navy and the Manhattan Project had to give sufficient priority to the project, and there would have to be "greater emphasis on Naval participation in design and construction of a Uranium pile reactor." Although the report enjoyed considerable enthusiastic response, the fact was that what Gunn and Abelson suggested was almost entirely theory and educated guess. No engineering had been done. At a briefing given by Abelson in 1946, a Navy attendee remembered thinking that "it sounded like something out of Jules Verne's *Twenty Thousand Leagues Under the Sea*."

Despite the report's call for greater naval participation in nuclear development, General Groves would not share nuclear information unless personnel were under his direct command. (During the war, several naval officers had held key positions in the Army-run Manhattan Project; two of those officers, William Parsons and Frederick Ashworth, had been the weapon officers, respectively, on the B-29s that dropped atomic bombs on Hiroshima and Nagasaki.)

Vice Admiral Bowen, who had recently been appointed to head the new Office of Research and Inventions, co-authored a letter sent by the Secretary of the Navy to the Secretary of War on March 14, 1946, seeking an increase in the Navy's role in atomic programs. In response, Secretary of War Robert Patterson advised that the Navy would best benefit by assigning personnel to the power-pile program being set up at Oak Ridge, Tennessee. With General Groves' approval, Patterson was willing to have a group of naval officers participate in the program to prepare for the eventual development of a shipboard reactor plant.

Admiral Edward L. Cochrane, Chief of the Bureau of Ships, agreed that the decision was the "soundest possible approach to the problem [of an experimental power pile] and will produce the fastest results." The admiral noted that "at least 4–5 years will elapse before it will be possible to install atomic energy in a naval ship for propulsion purposes."

By mid-1946, BuShips was involved in several nuclear-power projects. Industrial firms that had participated in the Manhattan Project expressed interest in power reactors, and even ship propulsion was mentioned. The General Electric Company had taken over operation of the plutonium-producing plant at Hanford, Washington, and had established the Knolls Atomic Power Laboratory in Schenectady, New York. GE proposed development of a nuclear plant suitable for powering a destroyer. BuShips reacted favorably, and General Groves was asked to authorize GE to commence design studies. BuShips also awarded contracts to firms for research into the properties of sodium-potassium alloys and their possible use as a heat-transfer medium, that is, to transfer heat from the steam-producing reactor (pile) to a turbine.

The Navy began to assign officers and civilian engineers to these projects. Captain Albert G. Mumma, head of the machinery design division of BuShips, made up a list of participating officers. Mumma selected Captain Harry Burris, who had performed an outstanding job in expediting the production of steam plants for destroyer escorts during the war, to be the senior naval officer at Oak Ridge. At the same time, Rickover was assigned as one of two naval officers to work with GE at Schenectady to develop a destroyer nuclear plant. Admiral Mills, who had been Rickover's wartime boss, approved Mumma's recommendations with one exception—Rickover was ordered to Oak Ridge and Burris to Schenectady.

Captain Mumma believed that Rickover's style would antagonize fellow officers as well as the Army and civilian communities at Oak Ridge. Admiral Mills, who fully understood Rickover's "personality problems," believed that his singlemindedness could overcome any bureaucratic difficulties.

When Rickover received his orders in May 1946, he is said to have collected every text on math, physics, and chemistry he could lay his hands on, and, until his departure for Washington, D.C., in preparation for the Oak Ridge assignment, he spent every possible moment studying. Upon his arrival in Washington, Rickover combed the BuShips files for any documents related to atomic matters. He also met with officials from GE who were discussing their nuclear destroyer proposal with BuShips leaders.

When Rickover arrived at Oak Ridge in late June 1946, he joined scores of military and industrial engineers, scientists, and planners who were working on or observing the Daniels nuclear reactor project. Also present were men from Westinghouse, GE, and Allis Chalmers, who would later participate in the development of the nuclear submarine.

Rickover was the senior Navy officer at Oak Ridge, and by September 1946 his team was assembled. Each officer had been told he was going to Oak Ridge to learn and to send in his own reports, but Rickover soon established that he was the head of the Navy group by arranging to write his fellow officers' fitness reports—the evaluation sheets that would greatly affect their future promotions.

He insisted that at least one member of his team attend each of the lectures and courses given in nuclear physics and chemistry, including the reactor classes nicknamed DOPE—Doctors of Pile Engineering—by Dr. Edward Teller. The team operated on "Rickover time," with evenings and weekends devoted to more study and review. Every aspect of nuclear technology, especially the Daniels project, was absorbed. Rickover missed no opportunity to increase his own knowledge, after having told Dr. Teller when he first met him, "I am stupid." But, as Teller began educating Rickover, the pupil became the teacher, and Rickover explained the value of nuclear energy for ship propulsion.

Rickover talked his way into a meeting of the Atomic Energy Commission's General Advisory Committee, where, by consensus, they determined that in perhaps twenty years there would be a real demonstration of useful power, and perhaps sometime later it could be available for specific practical purposes. Turning to a Navy colleague, Rickover exclaimed, "Jesus! Twenty years! By that time you'll be an admiral and I'll be pushing up daisies." He then proceeded to stand up and berate the scientist.

Rickover and his team visited other nuclear-related facilities. When he returned to Washington for duty in September 1947, he had more knowledge of non-weapon nuclear matters than any other naval officer. Meanwhile, the establishment of the Atomic Energy Commission (AEC), which took over all nuclear activities and programs from the Army's Manhattan Project on January 1, 1947, had led to delays in the Navy's efforts to initiate a nuclear submarine program. The AEC commissioners sought to undertake a major survey of U.S. interests and resources in the nuclear field before committing to specific nuclear programs, such as nuclear propulsion.[6]

Admiral Mills, who had become head of the Bureau of Ships in November 1946, was angry at the AEC for its decision. The Navy's leadership was ready to move ahead on designing and then building a nuclear submarine. On December 5, 1947, the Chief of Naval Operations, Fleet Admiral Chester W. Nimitz, had formally recommended a nuclear-propulsion program to the Secretary of the Navy, and it had been approved. Mills appointed Rickover as head of the nuclear propulsion "desk" in BuShips, and then as his liaison to the AEC, a position that soon led to Rickover's becoming head of nuclear propulsion within the AEC.

The pieces were in place for the design and construction of the world's first nuclear-propelled vehicle.

4

Building the *Nautilus*

By the end of 1945, many American scientists and engineers were discussing the possibility of nuclear submarines. A Navy Department report dated November 19, 1945—apparently based on Gunn-Abelson data—listed the advantages of nuclear "transformations," which estimated a yield of three billion BTUs per pound of nuclear fuel compared to 18,000 BTUs per pound of diesel oil.[7] The report listed these "outstanding characteristics" of nuclear propulsion:

1. Unlimited range.
2. Continuous submerged operation for weeks is possible with good living conditions.
3. High submerged and surface speeds.
4. No refueling at sea—an annual job.
5. No recharging of batteries.
6. More power available for same weight and volume.
7. A dry ship [i.e., no need to surface or use snorkel to charge batteries].

8.   Control and handling about like present submarines.
9.   Submarine clean and habitable [i.e., no diesel oil].
10.   Space distribution not unlike present arrangements, except forward section of submarine [forward of reactor] will be detachable for repair or replacement, and forward [torpedo] tubes may have to be sacrificed.
11.   Operation easier than with diesels.
12.   Operation of power plant expected to be reliable.

Two "disadvantages" were listed:

1.   Poisoned areas forward [reactor] cannot be entered by *any personnel* and all controls must be remote.
2.   No repairs in the forward [reactor] compartment can be made away from a specially tooled yard.

Many naval officers were talking about nuclear propulsion. At the Bikini atomic bomb tests in the summer of 1946, Lieutenant Commander Richard B. Laning, commanding the diesel submarine *Pilotfish*, talked about the feasibility of an atomic-powered submarine with Dr. George Gamow, a leading nuclear scientist. Gamow calculated that such a craft could achieve underwater speeds of thirty knots and would have to be twice the size of existing submarines. Such a craft could be developed, he said, "in ten years if we really put our heart into it." Laning immediately wrote a letter, through the chain of command, recommending a nuclear-propulsion program and volunteering to serve in it. Laning did not recall having received a response. (Laning would become the first commanding officer of the second nuclear submarine—the USS *Seawolf*—in 1957.)

Meanwhile, in Washington, scientists Ross Gun and Philip Abelson had completed their report, "Atomic Energy Submarine," in March 1946. Although, in retrospect, it had severe shortcomings, the report captured the imagination of many Navy men. In the fall of 1946, Admiral Nimitz asked the Submarine Officers Conference to address the subject of nuclear propulsion. The request led to a major report, completed on January 9, 1947, that stated:

> Present anti-submarine techniques and new developments in submarine design have rendered our present fleet submarines obsolete, offensively and defensively, to a greater degree than any other type [of warship]. The development of a true submarine capable of operating submerged for unlimited periods, appears to be probable within the next ten years, provided nuclear power is made available for submarine propulsion.

The report fully supported nuclear propulsion. It recommended a multi-phase program, including the construction of advanced, conventionally propelled submarines pending the design and development of nuclear power plants. In addition, it recommended that future diesel-electric submarines be configured for subsequent conversion to nuclear propulsion. The report estimated that the first nuclear submarines could be ready for sea by the mid-1950s. Nimitz approved the report the day after it was submitted to him.

With the solid knowledge that Captain Rickover and his team members had gained at Oak Ridge and from their visits to other nuclear-related facilities, the Navy was ready to proceed with nuclear propulsion. In his two-hat positions—head of nuclear propulsion with the Bureau of Ships and head of naval nuclear propulsion with the Atomic Energy Commission—created by Admiral Mills, Rickover was ready to proceed with the construction of a nuclear-propelled submarine, which Congress authorized for the fiscal year 1951 shipbuilding program.

American industry was anxious to enter the nuclear era, and the Navy soon established contracts with Westinghouse, General Electric, and Combustion Engineering for the development of suitable reactor plants. The prototypes of submarine plants would be constructed on land, to be used to model the shipboard installations, identify and correct problems, and train crews. Further, these prototype plants would be assembled within actual submarine hull sections, to save time and ensure the "fit" in actual submarines.

The early selection of a shipyard was necessary for the fabrication of hull sections for those reactor prototypes. The design department of the Portsmouth Naval Shipyard—the Navy's premier submarine yard—was fully engaged in the new *Tang*-class diesel submarines and the modernization of existing submarines under the so-called GUPPY program, as well as a variety of submarine conversions.[8] Rickover turned to the private Electric Boat (EB) yard, in Groton, Connecticut, which took on the detailed design and construction of the first U.S. nuclear submarines.

The planned nuclear submarine would use the fission of a reactor to heat water, much the same as a steam boiler does in oil-burning turbine ships. The submarine reactor would use pressurized water as the heat exchange medium between the reactor and the turbine. This was known as a Pressurized-Water Reactor (PWR), initially designated Submarine Thermal Reactor (STR) for the first nuclear submarine.[9] The STR Mark I would be the land prototype and the STR Mark II would be installed in the nuclear submarine, soon to be named *Nautilus*. The plants would be virtually identical.

Until about 1950 the first nuclear submarine was envisioned as exclusively a test submarine for a nuclear plant. Preliminary characteristics for the ship were noted: "Initially there will be no armament in the original [nuclear] ship, however, the design and construction should be such that armament . . . could be installed with a minimum of structural changes and at a minimum cost as a conversion project."

The EB design for the *Nautilus* provided for a larger submarine than had been envisioned in the 1950 BuShips study. The EB submarine would have a surface displacement of 3,180 tons and 3,500 tons submerged, with a length of almost 324 feet. This was almost half again the displacement of the postwar

Tang-class diesel submarine and more than fifty feet longer, the additional size being required for the nuclear plant.

The Mark I prototype of the *Nautilus* reactor plant was assembled at the national reactor test station near Arco in the Idaho desert. The hull section housing the reactor itself was constructed in a tank some fifty feet in diameter and almost forty feet high, holding some 385,000 gallons of water. With this arrangement, tests with the reactor compartment at sea could be simulated. Provided in adjacent hull sections were the heat exchanger, pumps, and a turbine. The reactor was built with the same massive lead shielding that would be fitted in the submarine. The 27-2/3–foot height of the reactor compartment (i.e., the submarine's inner or pressure hull diameter at that point) was dictated in part by the problem of control rods.

The control rods—fabricated of hafnium, a neutron-absorbing element—were raised to permit nuclear fission to occur and lowered to halt fission. The rods were screw-threaded and would be moved up and down by an electromagnetic field, operating a rotor on the top of each rod. (This screw concept would provide the crew with maximum safety from radiation in comparison with the pulley concept subsequently adopted for Soviet submarines.)

The Arco reactor plant achieved criticality—a self-sustained nuclear reaction—on March 30, 1953. Extensive tests followed, with problems uncovered and corrected. Then, in an impressive test in June 1953, the plant successfully undertook a ninety-six-hour "voyage," in theory, driving a submarine some 2,500 nautical miles across the Atlantic at an average speed of twenty-six knots.

The *Nautilus* herself was now under construction, and President Harry S. Truman officiated at the keel laying on June 14, 1952, at the Electric Boat yard. She was launched on January 21, 1954, when Mrs. Mamie Eisenhower broke the champagne bottle against the ship. Already under construction on an adjacent building way at Electric Boat was the second atomic submarine, the *Seawolf*, also begun in 1952. These historic events were marked by a blaze of publicity and were well-covered in the American and overseas press.

The *Nautilus* looked for the most part like an enlarged Type XXI U-boat with a rounded bow and streamlined hull and conning tower. Aft she had upper and lower rudders and twin screws. Her twenty-eight-foot beam and length provided a large interior volume, with three levels in most of the submarine. She had six compartments: bow, main living quarters and galley, central operating, reactor, engine room, and stern compartments.

Forward were six torpedo tubes with twenty-six torpedoes being carried (there were no stern tubes and, of course, no deck guns). A large BQR-4A passive sonar was fitted in the submarine's "chin" position, fully faired into the hull, with an SQS-4 active scanning sonar also fitted in the bow. There was briefly a thought of providing the *Nautilus* with a Regulus land-attack cruise missile; however, that idea was quickly rejected to avoid complications in producing the first nuclear submarine. (The Revell model company produced a *Nautilus* fitted with a Regulus hangar and fixed launching ramp aft of the sail structure.)

There were accommodations for twelve officers and just over ninety enlisted men; the officers shared staterooms, except for the captain, who had a private cubicle, and there was a separate wardroom where the officers could eat and relax. Each sailor had his own bunk, and the crew's mess could accommodate thirty-six men at one sitting for meals, or up to fifty for movies and lectures. The *Nautilus* had a built-in ice cream machine, Coca-Cola dispenser, and nickel-a-play jukebox connected to the ship's hi-fi system. Life on board would be luxurious by previous submarine standards because the nuclear plant would be able to provide unlimited fresh water and air conditioning.

Aft of the attack center and the control room (located on two levels beneath the sail structure), the after portion of the *Nautilus* was devoted to the propulsion plant and auxiliary machinery. The single STR reactor (later designated S2W) provided heat for the steam generators, which, in turn, provided steam to the two turbines. The plant produced 13,400 horsepower (less than the designed 15,000), enough to drive the large submarine at a maximum submerged speed of just over twenty-three knots.

At one point, according to Rickover, a twin-reactor plant

was considered to reduce the possibility that the submarine would be disabled or lost at sea because of a reactor failure. However, size was a constraint, and the *Nautilus* was built with only one reactor. The ship had an auxiliary diesel generator, complete with snorkel installation for submerged operation, and a battery installation to provide power to "bring home" the submarine in an emergency.

While deep-diving submarines demanded quality in materials and construction, the nuclear plant, with its radioactive and high-pressure steam components, demanded a new level of quality control. Rickover's mania for quality control in the *Nautilus* would establish a policy that would greatly enhance the safety record of U.S. nuclear submarines.

◆●×●◆

While the *Nautilus* was being constructed, on July 1, 1953, Rickover was selected for promotion to rear admiral at the specific direction of the Secretary of the Navy. Rickover had previously been "passed over" for promotion by Navy selection boards because of his acerbic personality, coupled with the small number of engineering officers that could be selected for flag rank— a percentage of the total number of officers that was set by law. Several of Rickover's staff, both officers and civilians, contacted members of Congress as well as the press in an effort to force the Navy to promote Rickover—and they were successful in their efforts. (Although he had renounced Judaism in 1931, his Jewish origins were often raised—incorrectly—as the reason for his non-promotion. An article in *Time* magazine by Clay Blair headlined "Brazen Prejudice" told of the prejudice against Rickover, but a careful reading of the piece revealed that it was prejudice within the Navy against engineering officers, not Jewish officers.)

The *Nautilus* was formally placed in commission on September 30, 1954, but she remained fast to the pier at the Electric Boat yard. The ceremony was for public relations purposes, to demonstrate that the Rickover organization had met its schedule. The submarine's reactor plant was started up on December 30 and on January 17, 1955, the *Nautilus* moved away from the pier. Despite a sudden engineering problem that was quickly solved as the submarine moved down the Thames River, her commanding officer, Commander Eugene P. Wilkinson, had a signal lamp flash the historic message: UNDERWAY ON NUCLEAR POWER.

The submarine's trials over the next few weeks were highly successful, including a record submerged run of 1,381 nautical miles from New London, Connecticut, to San Juan, Puerto Rico, in ninety hours—an average of 15.3 knots. This was the fastest submerged transit yet undertaken by a submarine. Subsequently, faster submerged passages were made, averaging close to her maximum speed. The *Nautilus* was a remarkable engineering achievement and a tribute to Admiral Rickover and his team.

In exercises, *Nautilus* demonstrated the value of nuclear propulsion for submarines. She could close with an enemy or escape at will, being maneuverable in three dimensions, regardless of surface weather conditions. She could even outrun available U.S. anti-submarine homing torpedoes. Unlike the captains of "high-speed" submarines of the Type XXI, GUPPY, or *Tang* submarines, the captain of the *Nautilus* did not have to concern himself with remaining battery power; he could steam at high speeds for days or even weeks, rather than hours or perhaps minutes.

The *Nautilus*, however, was a noisy submarine. Vortex shedding—the eddy or whirlpool motion of water behind the sail or fairwater structure—caused the sail structure to vibrate. At 180 cycles per minute, the sail vibration frequency came dangerously close to that of the natural tendency of the hull to flex or vibrate as it passed through the water. If the two frequencies came into harmony, the *Nautilus* could have suffered serious structural damage. In the process of exploring the sail vibration, Navy engineers uncovered "excessive" vibrations in the hull at speeds above sixteen knots.

Beyond the structural problems, these vibrations affected the submarine's performance. Commander Wilkinson wrote:

Noise generated by hull and superstructure vibration is so great that *Nautilus* sonar capability is practically nil at any speed over 8 knots. This intolerable situation reduces its military effectiveness sufficiently to materially restrict the tactical advantages inherent in nuclear power. Furthermore, it endangers the safety of the ship.

Modifications were made to remedy the *Nautilus*'s problems. But as Navy Department historian Gary Weir wrote: "Even with its destructive forward hull vibration eliminated, *Nautilus* remained notoriously loud and easily detected. Thus it became a floating operational laboratory for a wide variety of self-noise investigations." During the two years that the *Nautilus* was the world's only nuclear-propelled submarine, she proved to be a most valuable technical and tactical laboratory.

After several operations under the edge of the Arctic ice pack, and one aborted effort to sail under the ice to the North Pole, the *Nautilus* transited from Pearl Harbor to England, passing under the North Pole on August 3, 1958—the first ship ever to reach the "top" of the world. Under her second commanding officer, Commander William R. Anderson, the ship operated under the ice for four days, steaming 1,830 nautical miles. The polar transit was undertaken at the direct request of President Eisenhower, who was hoping to recapture the image of American technological leadership after the Soviet space triumphs of 1957–1958. Indeed, the mission was top secret until the submarine, having emerged from the ice, came to the surface near Iceland. There, a helicopter picked up Anderson, flew him to the U.S. air base in Iceland, and a transport plane whisked him to Washington, D.C., where he was decorated in a White House ceremony at which the president revealed the polar operation. Anderson was then flown back to his submarine for the triumphant entry of the *Nautilus* into Portland, England.

Upon her return to the United States, the *Nautilus* entered New York Harbor (at this writing, she was the only nuclear-propelled ship ever to have visited that city). The *Nautilus* continued in active Navy service as both a laboratory and an operational combat submarine until 1979. During her twenty-four years in commission, the *Nautilus* nuclear plant was refueled three times; on her four nuclear cores, here is how far she sailed:

> 1955–1957: 62,559.6 nautical miles, of which
> 36,498 nautical miles were submerged
> 1957–1959: 91,325 nautical miles
> 1959–1967: 174,507 nautical miles
> 1967–1979: 162,382 nautical miles

By a large margin, on her later nuclear cores almost all of the submarine's time at sea was submerged.

When the *Nautilus* was retired in 1979, the U.S. Navy had 113 nuclear-propelled submarines in service, plus several nuclear-propelled aircraft carriers and surface missile ships, and the nuclear-propelled research submersible *NR-1*. Admiral Rickover had created a nuclear navy.

5

Admiral of the Hill

I n July 1959, Vice President Richard M. Nixon flew to the Soviet Union, officially to open the American National Exhibition in Moscow and unofficially to launch himself as the kind of presidential candidate who could talk face-to-face with Soviet leader Nikita Khrushchev. The highly publicized trip was billed as Nixon's "Mission to Moscow," and although he did not wish to share that publicity with anyone, he did take along a small entourage that included Vice Admiral Rickover. He went along in a vague gesture of technical exchange, since a party of Soviet officials had recently visited the United States and Rickover had escorted them on part of their tour.

Also, the Soviet *Sputnik 1*, the first artificial earth satellite, had gone into orbit nearly two years before, and the Eisenhower administration was still smarting from having been "beaten by the Russians." Rickover's presence was a way of pointing out that at least the United States had built a nuclear submarine before the Soviets.

Although Rickover was hardly noticed during the trip, he had also launched himself on it. He would gain the capacity to speak to Congress on subjects beyond nuclear power; less than a month after his trip to the Soviet Union, he went before the House Committee on Appropriations and gave his "Report on Russia." Most of the lengthy session had to do with education although nuclear propulsion and his visit to the then-being-built icebreaker *Lenin*, the world's first nuclear-propelled surface ship, and submarines were also discussed.

Overnight, Rickover had become more than an admiral, more than an engineer. He was now a witness for much of what Congress wished to hear about, especially American education, which had been placed under a microscope following the orbiting of *Sputnik 1* in October 1957. His testimony before the congressional committee on August 18, 1959, which covered eighty single-spaced pages, addressed his views of what was wrong with American education and the American people, and why the Russians were pulling ahead. "If the father works a five-day week," Rickover testified, "if he wastes his leisure time, if he goes on long vacations, how can he expect to convince his children they ought to go to school six days a week for more than one hundred and eighty days a year?"

And so it went: what was wrong with foundations, with boards of education, with the American spirit? It was a lecture, a warning about "the Russian educational menace" and the need for America's post-*Sputnik* society to reform. He talked on and on, issuing personal proclamations based on his few days abroad, reeling off statistics on education in America, the Soviet Union, and wherever else he wished to draw comparisons between our decadent society and more sensible, more Spartan European societies. "For example, when you compare the years spent at school by a Danish child. . . ."

Rickover said that he was compelled to testify. "I have to take off time from my real work to be here," he told the congressmen. "I do not have a minute's time." He was setting himself up as a savior: if Congress, if the American people, would only listen to him, he could show the way to save the country. Much of his way would be through drastic changes in American education. He would make a separate crusade of that. But it would be from the pulpit of congressional hearing rooms that he would try to save America, and Congress could not get enough of him.

Rickover continued to testify regularly before congressional committees for the next two decades, increasing his number of appearances as he and the Congress waxed in their mutual admiration. By 1966 he was sitting at a witness table several times a year. By the time he went before committees of the Ninety-sixth Congress in 1979, he had been an official witness more than 150 times, with his staff having primed the representatives and senators before the hearings with specific questions that could showcase the admiral. He had spoken to members of Congress informally on innumerable other occasions.

Each time he walked into a hearing room and sat at the witness table before a Senate or House committee, he had scrupulously prepared himself—often with learned quotations and epigrams, a tool very few of his admiral colleagues ever employed, and one that tended to add credibility to his conclusions. He could testify as an expert witness on practically anything—on foreign relations, on morality, on management systems, on mediocrity in society, or on treaties ("Bismarck once said to an Austrian diplomat. . . .").

In one dazzling congressional performance, Rickover referred to or quoted Aristotle, Otto von Bismarck, Edmund Burke, Lewis Carroll, Rachel Carson, Catherine the Great, Winston Churchill, Hercules' cousin Eurystheus, Frederick the Great, Galileo, George Gallup, Adolf Hitler, Sherlock Holmes, Langston Hughes, William James, Thomas Jefferson, Carl Jung, Robert E. Lee, Douglas MacArthur, Thomas Babington Macaulay, Andre Malraux, George Marshall, William McKinley, Gregor Mendel, Count Metternich, Billy Mitchell, Napoleon, Richard M. Nixon, Elihu Root, Matthew Ridgway, Herbert Spencer, Josef Stalin, Voltaire, Max Weber, Woodrow Wilson, and Hyman G. Rickover.

Once a Congressman even asked Rickover about his "concept of man's purpose in life." The admiral did not hesitate to answer, beginning with a quotation from Voltaire and continuing for about three thousand more words. The Rickover Lecture, as it came to be called, would be set down in official records as

"Views" of Admiral Rickover, in contrast to, "Testimony" of a Chief of Naval Operations or "Statement" of a Deputy Secretary of Defense. The implication was that others spoke directly to specific issues and testified in the traditional way by giving answers to questions, while Rickover dispensed his views from a loftier vantage point. But there was always more to the Rickover Lecture than a voyage through his remarkable mind. No matter how far he might tack, he always stayed on course: what Rickover thought about the deficiencies of the U.S. Navy.

Rickover was doing more than fighting the system. He was building his own. Wherever the Navy was on any issue, Rickover was almost inevitably 180 degrees away. And he was always trying to convince the money-dispensers in Congress that he was on their side—against the "bureaucracy." Shrewdly, Rickover had sensed something that few others in the defense establishment had ever realized. He had discovered that members of Congress preferred to give money to people rather than to institutions. The Navy, like the Army and the Air Force, is only an abstraction. Members of Congress have to be patriotic and "support" the Army, Navy, and Air Force. But they do not have to like these institutions, which are represented by a parade of generals and admirals who come before them to plead for weapons, people, and bases. Because those officials change every couple of years, there is little opportunity to develop real relationships or understanding of personal views.

But Rickover thoroughly understood the congressional preference for supporting individuals. Accordingly, he came before congressional committees as an individual, not as a Navy official. He gave the strong and convincing impression that he spoke as a man speaking to them with total candor. Within all of the messages Rickover imparted to Congress was his fundamental theme: The Navy should become a nuclear navy run by Rickover, because he alone knew everything there was to know about nuclear power and about the Navy. Speaking, for instance, about the Navy's officer rotation policies, Rickover testified, "Perhaps the reason I can talk with a little more cogency on the subject is that I stick around. The other people come and go as on a conveyor belt."

Representative Daniel J. Flood, a power on the House Appropriations Committee, responded: "The only reason you stick around is because we insist you stick around or you would have been a dead duck long ago."

Rickover openly and proudly admitted to disobeying orders. "I have been importuned year after year by the Navy to undertake very expensive developments in nuclear power," he told Congress. "I have refused to undertake them because I could not see real promise in them." Those who "importuned" Rickover were his legal superiors, the Secretary of the Navy and the Chief of Naval Operations. Despite the words of his oath and commissions—"to obey the orders of those placed over me"—he could freely tell Congress, which granted such commissions, that he would refuse such orders so that he could be candid with them.

From the beginning of the nuclear program, Rickover realized that the ego and vanity of politicians were larger and hungrier than those of other mortal men. And he made offerings, such as submarine-collected bottles of polar water and chunks of polar ice. Members of Congress were given submarine-postmarked letters that said "At Sea. North Atlantic," which he sent to each member of a key committee every time he went to sea on a nuclear ship's trials.

He even dispensed immortality to the dead and the living. Once, tradition held that warships be named categorically: battleships for states of the Union; cruisers for cities; destroyers for men (and women) who benefited or served in the Navy and Marine Corps; aircraft carriers for historic ships or famous victories; and submarines for fish and other marine life. When the new category of Polaris missile submarines was created in 1958, President Eisenhower himself reportedly decided that those ships would be named for famous Americans—*George Washington*, *Patrick Henry*, and *Theodore Roosevelt* were the first three of those forty-one ballistic missile submarines.

In 1969, with strong White House support, the Navy began naming large destroyer-type ships, called "frigates," in the U.S. Navy, for states. Previously those ships, designated DLG and DLGN if nuclear, were named for naval heroes and leaders—Truxtun, Fox, Biddle, Bainbridge, etc. The first with a state name, a name source previously used for battleships, was the USS *California*, honoring the home state of the incumbent president, Richard Nixon. When the *California*'s keel was laid down on January 23, 1970, it was "authenticated" by the wife of Glenard P. Lipscomb, ranking Republican member of the House Appropriations Committee's defense subcommittee. A week later, on February 1, 1970, Lipscomb died. Rickover named a submarine for him, a man who was another supporter of his programs.

Traditionally, ship names were chosen by the Secretary of the Navy, based mainly upon the recommendations of his Director of Naval History. William H. Bates, representative from Massachusetts, had served on the Joint Committee on Atomic Energy since 1959 and was a strong Rickover supporter. When the carrier *John F. Kennedy* was launched in 1967, it was Bates who, on the floor of the House, declared: "It is a sad commentary for those who have worked for the development of nuclear propulsion in our Navy to see a ship which will be with us in the year 2000 will be propelled by conventional means, and not nuclear propulsion."

In 1970, a nuclear attack submarine under construction at the Ingalls shipyard in Pascagoula, Mississippi, was named *William H. Bates*. It broke the seventy-year tradition of naming submarines for marine life, for not since the U.S. Navy's first submarine, the USS *Holland*, placed in service in 1900, had a torpedo-armed or "attack" submarine been named for a person. More followed, as time took a toll on Rickover supporters and he was able to dispense a new kind of largess. An admiral put the reason for the change in the tradition of naming submarines in three words: "Fish don't vote." Subsequent attack submarines named after politicians who supported nuclear programs were the *L. Mendel Rivers*, for the late chairman of the House Armed Services Committee, and the *Richard B. Russell*, for the chairman of the Senate Armed Services Committee.

The White House stepped in at that point and, to gain more political support, began naming submarines for cities, a traditional name source for cruisers. Thus, the next attack submarine was the USS *Los Angeles*, completed in 1976.

At virtually all ceremonies for these nuclear submarines, as well as for nuclear-propelled carriers and cruisers—which occurred every couple of days when one considered that each warship had a festive keel laying, launching, and commissioning—Rickover, never in uniform, would be on stage, front and center. Always, at the last minute, he would rearrange the seating; bow graciously and say just the right words to the ladies, and their children or grandchildren when present; joke with the congressional delegation; and avoid most—or all—Navy and shipyard officials. It was always Congress first, and at times Congress only.

By the 1970s, Rickover was practically an honorary member of Congress and was proud of his longevity, at times even touched by it. When he walked into the Joint Committee's hearing room on February 25, 1974, he carried a list of members who had been on the committee in previous years. With his usual precision, he named them in alphabetical order, from William Bates to Arthur Vandenberg. He had known them all, and they all were dead. He was a man so old, so long in office, that he was seemingly defying a fundamental law of nature: Here was a man who was, in some respects, older than the Congress. And here was the secret of his success on Capitol Hill: Hang on. It was not really a secret, though. At a naval aviation luncheon in Washington, he was asked publicly, "How do you get things done?" He answered: "You just outlive them."

His supreme achievement as "Admiral of the Hill" was the passage of the unique piece of legislation in 1974 that stipulated all major combat ships of the strike forces of the Navy had to be nuclear-powered.[10] This made the creation of an all-nuclear navy—a Rickover navy—a matter of law, which said there could be only one way a non-nuclear ship could be built: the president would have to advise Congress and say that a certain ship had to be powered by something other than a Rickover reactor because such a non-nuclear ship was "in the national interest." Such a ship, to the lawmakers, was unimaginable, and such a humiliating act by the Commander in Chief was also unimaginable.

The law had been long in coming. Mention of an all-nuclear navy had been made by Rickover's congressional supporters as far back as his first promotion fight in 1953. In the 1960s, the concept of a nuclear navy came up again and again in Rickover's Capitol Hill bastions—the Joint Committee on Atomic Energy and the House Armed Services Committee, and men whose names would be on submarines showed up again and again as champions of the nuclear navy. They orated passionately in Congress. They tirelessly wrote long, and often angry, politically threatening letters to the president, the Secretary of Defense, and high-ranking Navy officials.

But their most important battle, the one that rallied them, was one they lost. That was in 1967 when the carrier *John F. Kennedy* was launched. She was not nuclear-powered, and the nuclear-power zealots in Congress vowed that this would never happen again.

Representative Daniel J. Flood attacked Secretary of Defense Robert S. McNamara and "Mr. McNamara's Band at the Pentagon" for making "one of the most shocking errors and mistakes in the history of our Military Establishment." Flood said that never again would he vote for a combat ship that was not nuclear-powered. Armed Services Committee Chairman L. Mendel Rivers said that as long as he held that post, there never would be a carrier that was oil-powered. To underscore its concern, Congress ordered the Secretary of the Navy to design and build as soon as possible two nuclear-powered missile frigates (DLGNs) to operate with carriers.[11]

On February 13, 1976—less than two years after the all-nuclear legislation—President Gerald Ford formally made a finding that constructing an all-nuclear surface combatant force was not in the national interest. It was the Secretary of Defense's assessment that the military value of an all-nuclear powered warship program did not warrant the increased costs or, alternatively, the reduced force levels. After that date, only one more nuclear DLGN/cruiser was built, although nuclear-propelled carrier construction continued in addition to an all-nuclear submarine force.

In this period, Rickover's power base in Congress began to dissipate as several of his strongest supporters passed away or retired. Also, the Atomic Energy Commission and the Joint Committee on Atomic Energy were dismantled. In January 1977, the

House Armed Services Committee was given authority over the national security programs of the Energy Research and Development Administration (the predecessor to the Department of Energy and the Nuclear Regulatory Commission). The Armed Services Committee formed the Subcommittee on Intelligence and Military Applications of Nuclear Energy, and it was before this committee—the mere shadow of the powerful Joint Committee—that Rickover appeared for the first time on April 27, 1977.

Rickover began testifying in his age-old way, answering perhaps a few more questions than he had been used to, and hearing some mild contradictions to his answers. There was just the slightest hint that some of the new members did not quite feel about Rickover the way their predecessors had. His testimony was suddenly ended when a congressman told Rickover, "We have a vote here."

"Are you coming back, sir?" Rickover asked.

"No, Admiral," replied Representative Charles H. Wilson of California, a member of Congress since 1962. "I think we are going to recess the committee now and we want to express our great appreciation to you for coming and assisting us today."

"I hope I have your permission to extend my remarks and to complete my testimony," Rickover said.

"Absolutely. Your entire statement and any accompanying material that you may want to submit in connection with it, backup material, will be made a part of the record."

"Thank you, sir."

"We appreciate it very much," Wilson said. He appeared nervous, perhaps embarrassed. "Thank you very much. We will recess the hearing."

Rickover was left to put the rest of his statement into the printed record. It began, "As you know, I have been responsible for directing the naval nuclear propulsion program for over twenty-eight years . . . ."

He was still Admiral of the Hill, although perhaps he was not viewed that way by as many members as he had once known.

6

The Rickover Navy

By 1956—a little more than one year after the USS *Nautilus* had gone to sea—the U.S. Navy's leadership made the decision to stop constructing diesel-electric submarines. That decision meant that the Navy would seek an undersea fleet that was almost completely propelled by nuclear power plants developed by Admiral Rickover. The Navy's long-term blueprint for the future fleet, a policy paper entitled *The Navy of the 1970 Era* and dated January 13, 1958, provided for 127 submarines by the 1970s:

> 40 Polaris ballistic missile submarines (1,500-nautical-mile missile range)
> 12 cruise missile submarines (1,000-nautical-mile missile range)
> 75 torpedo-attack (anti-submarine) submarines

All but ten of the attack submarines were to have nuclear propulsion. Those ten were newly built diesel-electric submarines, which would serve in the fleet for many years (the last was retired in 1990 after thirty years of service).

When the *Nautilus* went to sea in January 1955, the Navy already had her sister ship, the *Seawolf*, under construction, with several additional nuclear submarines in the planning stage. Indeed, Rickover was already planning a "family" of nuclear power plants for those submarines as he sought to find the configuration that would provide the most efficient (for speed) but also the safest plants that could be produced.

For the *Seawolf*, Rickover developed a nuclear plant employing liquid sodium in place of water as the heat exchange medium between the reactor and propulsion turbine. Sodium offered the promise of a more efficient heat exchange; hence, more power could be transferred to the turbine to produce higher speeds. But sodium was toxic and highly corrosive. Again, Rickover built a prototype of the sodium nuclear plant—officially the Submarine Intermediate Reactor (SIR)—for the *Seawolf* at West Milton, New York. Later designated S1G, it was used for development and crew training. The almost-identical SIR Mark II plant (S2G) was installed in the *Seawolf*. Unfortunately, materials technology was not at a level to support the effects of sodium, and when the *Seawolf* went to sea in January 1957, after many delays, she was never able to reach her promised performance.

Under Commander Richard (Dick) Laning, the *Seawolf* operated primarily in anti-submarine exercises. On September 26, 1957, President Eisenhower became the first U.S. chief executive to go to sea in a nuclear submarine, as the *Seawolf* cruised off the New England coast.

There were periodic problems with the plant—and some unusual phenomena. Sometimes, for example, the *Seawolf*'s hull would glow in the dark. The light was Cherenkov radiation, a bluish glow emitted by high-speed charged particles as they pass from one medium to another.[12] The radiation, more commonly observed in the water around a nuclear reactor, was not dangerous, but it was novel.

The *Seawolf* demonstrated the underwater endurance of nuclear submarines in the fall of 1958 when Laning took her on a record-breaking submerged run of 13,761 nautical miles,

"Rickie" as Rickover appeared in the 1922 edition of *Lucky Bag,* the yearbook of the Naval Academy. Although that *Lucky Bag* contained an unnumbered perforated page for another Jewish midshipman, Rickover and his classmate Louis Goodman shared a permanent, numbered page in the yearbook.

Ruth Masters Rickover. (*Courtesy U.S. Naval Academy*)

Rickover, in uniform, astride a carabao, or water buffalo, while in Bali. Rickover and his wife Ruth Masters made an extensive tour of Southeast Asia in 1938, which led to her writing a charming and perceptive book, published after her death under Rickover's sponsorship. (*Courtesy of U.S. Naval Institute*)

Vice Admiral Earle Mills provided the power and authority behind Rickover during his early days of the nuclear-propulsion program. Mills had been Rickover's boss in the Bureau of Ships during World War II. (*U.S. Navy*)

President Truman initials the keel plate for the *Nautilus* on June 14, 1952. Immediately behind him are John Jay Hopkins, chairman and president of General Dynamics Corp.; O. Pomeroy Robinson, general manager of Electric Boat; and Secretary of the Navy Dan Kimball. Rickover is behind Hopkins and Rickover's son, Robert, is behind him. (*Electric Boat*)

President Eisenhower—accompanied by the press—takes the controls on his second trip in a nuclear submarine, the USS *Patrick Henry*, in 1960. Earlier, he rode the nuclear submarine *Seawolf*. Every president afterward up to Jimmy Carter rode a nuclear submarine with Rickover in attendance, pointing out the value of such craft. (*U.S. Navy*)

Commander Eleonore Bednowicz, Rickover's second wife. A career navy nurse, she retired shortly after her marriage to Rickover. (*U.S. Navy*)

One of the very few occasions when Rickover appeared in the uniform of a full admiral took place on March 29, 1974, when Rickover Hall was dedicated at the U.S. Naval Academy. From left are Mrs. Rickover, Rickover, and Congresswoman Marjorie Holt. Also in the official party was Secretary of the Navy John Warner, subsequently a U.S. senator; he directed Rickover to wear his uniform for the occasion. (*U.S. Navy*)

President Carter and Rickover after the president's first visit to a nuclear submarine, the USS *Los Angeles*, in 1977. Although Carter, a Naval Academy graduate, began nuclear power training, he left the Navy before completing the course. Rickover rarely appeared in uniform after the 1950s. (*U.S. Navy*)

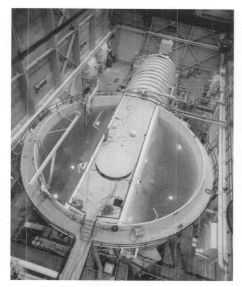

The first submarine nuclear power plant—the Submarine Thermal Reactor Mark I—was constructed in the Idaho desert at the national reactor test station. The prototype plant was within a submarine-like hull structure that passes through a water tank some fifty feet in diameter and forty feet high, holding about 385,000 gallons of water. (*Westinghouse*)

A ticker-tape welcome was given to the crew of the *Nautilus* when the submarine reached New York after her Arctic exploit. Here Commander William R. Anderson (left), then commanding officer of the submarine, Richard C. Patterson, Jr., a New York City official, and Rear Admiral Rickover ride to City Hall, with the submarine's crew following in a convoy of jeeps. (*U.S. Navy*)

Rickover—in khaki uniform with black tie—stands on the port diving plane of the nuclear submarine *Barb* as she returned from her initial sea trials. The *Barb*, a *Thresher*-class submarine, has a narrow sail structure to house the retractable periscopes, antennas, and snorkel mast; there is no "conning tower" familiar to World War II submarines. (*Litton/Ingalls Shipbuilding*)

The USS *Thresher* was the first nuclear submarine to be lost. With the death of 129 men, this remains history's worst submarine disaster. Subsequently the USS *Scorpion* was lost, as were several Soviet-Russian nuclear submarines. The *Scorpion*, in addition to her nuclear reactor, carried two of the Mark 45 ASTOR nuclear-tipped torpedoes. (*U.S. Navy*)

The recently completed Polaris submarine *Sam Rayburn* waits with her sixteen missile tube hatches open while workmen finish the craft. Although diesel-electric propulsion is feasible for ballistic missile submarines—as built by the Soviet Union—nuclear propulsion adds to their effectiveness and survivability. (*Newport News Shipbuilding*)

A rare photo of a surface launching of a Polaris missile from the USS *Henry Clay* in 1964. Minutes earlier the submarines had launched a missile while submerged. Although Rickover was excluded from participating in the design of the Polaris submarines, his nuclear-propelled submarine program provided the basis for the U.S. sea-based strategic deterrence. (*U.S. Navy*)

Hail to the conquering heroes: The USS *Nautilus* steams up the East River toward the New York Naval Shipyard (Brooklyn)—the only time that a nuclear ship visited Gotham City. The visit came after her voyage to the North Pole. (*U.S. Navy*)

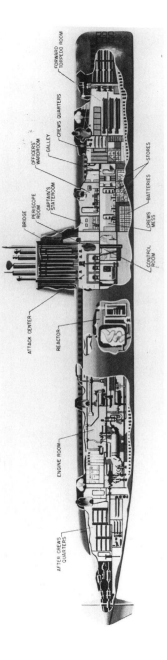

A cutaway view of the USS *Nautilus*. Her hull configuration was based on the German Type XXI submarine, the most advanced submarine design to enter service in World War II. (*U.S. Navy*)

The USS *Finch* was Rickover's only ship command. The minesweeper, launched in 1918, was well overage in 1937 when Rickover took command of her in Chinese waters. The *Finch* was being employed to transport American troops during the Sino-Japanese conflict. (*U.S. Navy*)

Rear Admiral Rickover aboard the USS *Nautilus*. (*U.S. Navy*)

remaining underwater for sixty consecutive days. The *Seawolf* operated successfully until late 1958 when she returned to the Electric Boat yard. She was torn open, her sodium plant was removed, and a duplicate of the *Nautilus* PWR plant was installed. She returned to service on September 30, 1960. "Overriding technical and safety considerations indicated the abandonment of the sodium-cooled reactor as a means for propelling naval ships," according to Rickover. A second reactor core was available for the *Seawolf,* and the Bureau of Ships as well as Laning recommended that the submarine be refueled (a three-month process compared to almost two years for replacing the sodium plant with a water plant) because of the demand for the early nuclear submarines for fleet anti-submarine training. But Rickover had, on his own authority, already directed that the spare *Seawolf* fuel core be cut up to reclaim the uranium. While many participants in the nuclear program, including Rickover, considered the sodium reactor a failure, one must keep in mind that progress could not be made without such attempts.

With her new pressurized-water plant, the *Seawolf* continued in service until early 1987, with most of the later stages of her career being spent in classified research, intelligence, and seafloor recovery work, including sending out divers to tap into Soviet seafloor communication cables.

Meanwhile, the Navy was entering the nuclear propulsion era on two tracks. First, Rickover deemed it necessary to develop multiple types of reactor plants, what would later be called "pushing the envelope." In this respect, he initiated—with strong congressional support—a small nuclear plant intended for a small, anti-submarine or "hunter-killer" submarine (the *Tullibee*); a large, two-reactor submarine plant intended to develop concepts for surface ship plants (the *Triton*); and a high-speed, S5W reactor plant, intended for a submarine with a speed in excess of thirty knots (the *Skipjack*).

The small reactor plant was not pursued beyond the submarine *Tullibee* (completed in 1960). The reactor plant and the submarine both grew in size as they were being designed and constructed. The resulting craft was felt to be limited in capability, and the new, high-speed attack submarines were believed to be better than the *Tullibee* for anti-submarine warfare. The twin-reactor plant was installed in the *Triton*. With a length of 447½ feet, she was the largest submarine yet constructed by any nation. She was a radar picket, intended to steam ahead of carrier task forces; upon detecting approaching enemy aircraft, the *Triton* would flash a warning to friendly forces and then submerge. Of course, once underwater the submarine could neither use her radar nor effectively communicate by radio.

The radar picket submarine concept—and several conventional submarines were built and converted for that role—evolved from World War II operations in the Pacific, when Japanese suicide planes attacked radar picket destroyers that were posted around U.S. carrier task forces. But even as the *Triton* was completed in 1959, the radar submarine program was being cut back, the submarines' role being overtaken by radar-carrying aircraft, which could "see" farther and could continue to operate effectively as the enemy planes closed on the task force. The *Triton* never operated in the radar picket role.

In 1959, the United States was smarting from a series of Soviet space and missile successes. In late January 1960, *Triton*'s commanding officer, Captain Edward L. Beach, was ordered to a top-secret meeting in Washington.[13] There he was informed that the *Triton* was being sent on an underwater, around-the-world cruise, essentially following the course of Ferdinand Magellan's ships (1519–1522). Such a trip would make important contributions to geophysical and oceanographic research, and help to determine the problems of long-duration operations—all important to the new Polaris submarine program. However, like the Arctic cruises of the *Nautilus* and other submarines, the around-the-world cruise was also looked at as a means of demonstrating U.S. technological excellence in the face of continuing Soviet space successes.

On February 16, 1960, the *Triton* departed New London with 184 officers, enlisted men, and civilian technicians on board. Steaming south, the *Triton* was forced to broach her sail above the surface on March 5 to permit a sailor who was seriously ill with kidney stones to be taken off near Montevideo and transferred to a U.S. cruiser.[14] The submarine rounded Cape Horn, sailed across the Pacific and Indian Oceans, rounded the Cape of Good Hope, and steamed northward. On May 2, Beach again broached the sail to take aboard two officers from a U.S. destroyer off Cadiz. During the cruise, the *Triton* was able to maintain continuous radio reception through the use of a buoyant floating cable antenna.

The *Triton* surfaced completely for the first time in eighty-three days, nineteen hours on May 10, off the coast of Delaware. A helicopter lifted Captain Beach from her deck and flew him to Washington where, at a White House ceremony, President Eisenhower revealed the voyage. Captain Beach was presented with an award, as were others in the submarine program. Admiral Rickover was neither invited to the White House ceremony nor was he mentioned in the speeches. To Rickover, this was a slight for which he never forgave the Navy's senior leaders who were responsible for the list of attendees at the White House.

Beach was then flown back to the *Triton* and was on board the next morning when the submarine tied up at New London. She had traveled 35,979 nautical miles submerged. The *Triton*'s achievements, however, were overshadowed in the news by the shooting down of a *U-2* spyplane piloted by Francis Gary Powers over the Soviet Union on May 1.

Subsequently, the *Triton* carried out routine operations. There were proposals to modify her to serve as an underwater command ship (for a naval commander or, in an emergency, for the president), or a "tug" to assist other submarines trapped under the Arctic ice pack, or a secret-operations submarine, but those proposals came to naught and she was permanently taken out of service in March 1969 after a decade of service.

Meanwhile, the United States had embarked on a remarkable nuclear submarine program to carry the Polaris Submarine-Launched Ballistic Missile (SLBM). A U.S. SLBM program was initiated in the aftermath of the Soviet detonation of a hydrogen (thermo-nuclear) device in August 1954 and the Big Four summit meeting in Geneva in September 1955. As a result of anticipated Soviet advances in strategic missiles, the Secretary of Defense directed the Navy to join the Army in development of an intermediate-range ballistic missile that could be launched from surface ships.

The Navy objected strenuously to the joint program, as the Army was developing the liquid-propellant Jupiter missile. The Navy considered liquid propellants too dangerous to handle at sea, and the fifty-five-foot missile would be difficult to install in ships. In addition, there was a general opposition to ballistic missiles at sea within the Navy from the "cultural" viewpoint on two issues: First, since the late 1940s, both the Bureau of Aeronautics and the Bureau of Ordnance were (separately) developing guided (cruise) missiles that could be launched from submarines against land targets; these organizations did not wish to give up their projects. Second, the Navy had lost the B-36 bomber versus carrier controversy to the Air Force in the late 1940s. That loss had cost the Navy prestige, plus cancellation of the first postwar aircraft carrier. As a result, the Navy's leadership wanted to avoid another interservice battle, this time over strategic missiles. Indeed, Admiral Robert B. Carney, Chief of Naval Operations from 1953 to 1955, had placed restrictions on the Navy's advocating the development of sea-based ballistic missiles. There was a third issue, which although not "cultural" to the Navy, was very real. This was the fear of having to pay for the SLBM development out of the regular Navy budget, which would require a cut in conventional weapon programs.[15]

The opposition to developing a sea-based ballistic missile force ended with the appointment of Admiral Arleigh A. Burke as Chief of Naval Operations in August 1955. According to Admiral Burke's biographer, "Burke's most significant initiative during his first term [1955–57] was his sponsorship, in the face of considerable opposition, of a high-priority program to develop a naval intermediate-range ballistic missile."[16]

Fearing that the project would be given low priority within the Navy and doomed to failure if left to the existing Navy bureaucracy, Admiral Burke established the Special Projects Office (SPO) to provide a "vertical" organization, separate from the existing technical bureaus, for directing the sea-based missile project. Previously, all major naval technical developments, as well as production, had been directed by the technical bureaus, a horizontal organizational structure that dated from 1842. In these moves he was strongly supported by the Secretary of the Navy, Charles S. Thomas.

Thus the Navy began looking at a Jupiter-based SLBM. The Navy still had severe misgivings about the use of highly volatile liquid propellants aboard ship and studies were initiated into solid-propellant missiles. However, solid-propellants had a low specific impulse or thrust ratio, a major shortcoming. The biggest boost for solid-propellants came in mid-1956 when scientists found it feasible to miniaturize thermo-nuclear warheads. Dr. Edward Teller is said to have suggested in the summer of 1956 that a four hundred–pound warhead could provide the explosive force of a five thousand–pound one.[17] In September, the Atomic Energy Commission estimated that a small nuclear warhead would be available by 1965, with an even chance of its being ready by 1963.

This development, coupled with the parallel development of higher specific impulse solid-fuel propellants, permitted: (1) a break from the Army's Jupiter program in December 1956, (2) formal initiation of the Polaris SLBM program with a solid-propellant missile, and (3) a shift from surface ships to submarines as the launch platform. On February 8, 1957, Admiral Burke issued a requirement for a 1,500–nautical mile missile launched from a submarine to be operational by 1965. A range of some 1,500 nautical miles was stipulated to permit a submarine in the Norwegian Sea to target the Soviet capital of Moscow—some 1,100 nautical miles inland.

The February 1957 schedule with a goal of 1965 was soon followed by a series of revisions and accelerations in the Polaris program. On October 4, 1957, the Soviets orbited *Sputnik 1*; on October 23 the Secretary of the Navy proposed acceleration of Polaris to provide a 1,200–nautical mile missile by December

1959, three SLBM submarines available by mid-1962, and a 1,500–nautical mile missile available by mid-1963. A month later the program was further accelerated to provide the 1,200–nautical mile missile by October 1960, and in December 1957, a plan was drawn up to provide the first submarine in December 1959, and the second in March 1960.

To produce the submarines in so short a time, on the last day of 1957 the Navy reordered a recently begun, nuclear-propelled, torpedo-attack submarine and a second, not-yet-started unit as ballistic missile submarines. Sections totaling 130 feet were added to the submarines for sixteen large missile tubes and special navigation and fire control equipment. Rickover's involvement in the Polaris program was minimal. The Rickover "issue" was handled astutely by Rear Admiral William F. "Red" Raborn, the head of the Polaris program, and by Admiral Burke's simple direction that the Polaris submarines would use the *Skipjack*'s S5W nuclear reactor plant. Additionally, according to AEC historians Richard Hewlett and Francis Duncan, "under written orders from Admiral Burke [Raborn and other admirals] excluded Rickover from all the preliminary studies."[18] Raborn and the other admirals involved in the Polaris project feared Rickover's participation "would lead to domination of the new project" by his office.[19]

Given the highest national priorities, the first Polaris submarine, the *George Washington*, was rushed to completion. The submarine fired the first submarine-launched Polaris missile on June 9, 1959. After outfitting and training, the submarine departed on the first strategic missile patrol on November 15, 1960. The submarine was armed with sixteen Polaris A-1 missiles with a range of 1,200 nautical miles, each carrying a warhead of almost one megaton. The *George Washington* was at sea on that initial patrol for sixty-seven consecutive days, remaining submerged for sixty-six days and ten hours to establish an underwater endurance record.

Before the *George Washington* returned to port, the second Polaris submarine, the *Patrick Henry*, had sailed on the second deterrent patrol on December 30, 1960. Additional Polaris submarines went to sea at regular intervals, with all forty-one submarines, carrying 656 missiles, being completed by 1967. Up to one-half of the force could be at sea at any given time, two alternating crews being assigned to each Polaris submarine. In several respects, the Polaris was a remarkable weapon system.

And, Rickover's nuclear-propulsion program had provided the basis for the Polaris and its successor SLBM programs—improved Polaris missiles, the Poseidon missile, and the Trident missiles.

7

Dangerous: Radiation Hazard

Admiral Rickover's most improbable magic trick involved the transformation of a nuclear reactor meant for an aircraft carrier into the nation's first reactor devoted to powering an electrical generating plant. The trick got Rickover into the world of commercial nuclear power, with mixed results for him and electrical utility companies.

The saga began with the outbreak of the Korean War in June 1950, when the value of aircraft carriers became dramatically apparent. All major airfields in South Korea were quickly overrun by communist troops, and bases in Japan were too far from the Korean Peninsula to permit effective fighter operations in the war zone. Less than two months after the start of the war, Admiral Forrest P. Sherman, Chief of Naval Operations, wrote a secret memorandum to his principal deputies and the Chief of BuShips: "I believe the time has come to explore the feasibility of constructing a large carrier with an atomic power plant to determine time factors, cost factors and characteristics."

Rickover's Naval Reactors Branch (NRB) reacted quickly, getting feasibility reports to Sherman within weeks. By December

1950, Sherman asked the Joint Chiefs of Staff, then the policy-making group within the Department of Defense, to "formally request the Atomic Energy Commission to consider undertaking now the construction of a shore-based prototype for aircraft carrier propulsion." The AEC assigned responsibility for monitoring the effort to another group in the division of reactor development, not to Rickover's NRB. Lawrence R. Hafstad, director of reactor development in AEC, feared that Rickover would simply scale up the submarine-reactor design to produce the carrier reactor. But Rickover, as usual, was working behind the scene, convincing important members of Congress to nudge the Joint Chiefs. In October 1951, the Chiefs approved a formal requirement for "a single shore-based prototype of a nuclear-powered propulsion unit suitable for driving one shaft of a major warship such as an aircraft carrier, and for use after completion of the shore installation for the production of plutonium and electric power."

Thus, the proposed carrier reactor could meet several goals: large-ship propulsion, plutonium for use in weapons, and a prototype for civilian power reactors. And, Rickover's NRB took control of the program. It seemed doomed when newly elected President Eisenhower cut the carrier out of the budget. Eisenhower, however, said he would consider any recommendation that the AEC would make for converting the program to the civilian role. Through this loophole, the AEC and Rickover pushed a proposal for the large-ship reactor design to become the prototype for a civilian power reactor.

The Duquesne Light Company of Pittsburgh offered to contribute $5 million toward the cost of the reactor, pay for the steam produced, build and operate the electric generating plant, operate the reactor after the AEC built it, and provide the site: Shippingport, a small town on the Ohio River, about twenty-five miles west of Pittsburgh. Ground was broken at Shippingport on September 6, 1954. Eventually, the 750-man work force would be on a sixty-hour week, with Rickover on the scene during many of those hours.

On December 2, 1957, exactly fifteen years after Enrico Fermi and his team of physicists at the University of Chicago produced the world's first sustained nuclear chain reaction, Shippingport's nuclear reactor achieved criticality. Sixteen days later, the reactor's steam-driven turbine was synchronized with the main generator, and soon electric power was flowing over Duquesne Light Company lines at full power— 60,000 kilowatts.

The company now had a nuclear power plant to operate. But, acting on his own, Rickover had insisted on an agreement that "at any time the plant was operating one of my representatives could be present in the control room with authority to shut the plant down if he thought it was not being operated safely." The "whole reactor game hangs on a much more slender thread than most people are aware," Rickover had said a few months before the Shippingport reactor went critical. "There are a lot of things that can go wrong and it requires eternal vigilance. All we have to have is one good accident in the United States and it might set the whole game back for a generation. We do not want that to happen."

Accidents did happen, and Rickover put as much distance as possible between them and him. During the night of April 9– 10, 1963, the USS *Thresher,* the lead ship of a new class of nuclear attack submarines, headed into the deep Atlantic off Boston. At 6:35 on the morning of April 10, with the submarine rescue ship *Skylark* standing by, the *Thresher* dove to her maximum operating, or test, depth. Some forty times before she had been to that depth. At the time, the Navy classified all information on submarine depths beyond four hundred feet, but, in view of subsequent statements by Navy officials, the *Thresher*'s test depth was 1,300 feet. In theory, U.S. submarines are designed to have a 50 percent safety margin over their test depth. That means if a problem forces a submarine below its operating depth, it should be safe for half again that distance. After that, the tremendous sea pressure (445 pounds per square inch at one thousand feet) will force sea fittings and pipes to fail, and then rupture the steel pressure hull.

As the *Thresher* plunged into the depths, she maintained communications with the *Skylark.* The messages did not mention the submarine's actual depths—in case Soviet intelligence craft or submarines were in the area. The dive was slow and careful, halting periodically while the crew and specialists checked equipment and instruments. At 9:02 A.M. the *Thresher* asked for a repetition of a course reading from the *Skylark*. Ten minutes later, the two ships made another routine check.

Then, "about a minute later," according to *Skylark*'s navigator, Lieutenant (junior grade) James Watson, the *Thresher* reported: "Have positive up angle. . . . Attempting to blow up." Others later said they heard, "Experiencing minor problem. . . . Have positive angle. . . . Attempting to blow." Or, "Experiencing minor difficulty. . . . Have positive up angle. . . . Attempting to blow. . . . Will keep you informed."

Those aboard the *Skylark* then heard the sounds of air under high pressure, as if a submarine were trying to "blow up" by using high-pressure air to force water out of her ballast tanks. Nothing more was heard from the submarine until 9:17 A.M., when there was a garbled message. One listener said the message was unintelligible; another said he heard the distinct words "test depth." Seconds later, Watson heard a sound he remembered from his World War II service: "the sound of a ship breaking up . . . like a compartment collapsing."

It was history's worst submarine disaster: a U.S. nuclear submarine had carried 129 men to their deaths.[20] The water depth where the *Thresher* was lost was 8,400 feet. Long before the submarine hit bottom, pipes and fittings had given way, admitting high-pressure jets of water to several compartments; moments later, the hardened steel hull began to pull, like taffy. The added weight of inrushing water pushed the submarine deeper at a still greater speed. Then, the tremendous water pressure imploded the submarine and blew in the unflooded spaces. The compression created a flash of heat and light. All men on board—some possibly already dead or injured from the inrushing water and pressure—died instantly.

The remains of the *Thresher* rained down on the ocean floor.

That night, Admiral Rickover made several telephone calls. One was to the Office of Information, where he advised the naval officers on duty that he was available for any help that they may need from him. He also called Vice Admiral Ralph K. James, Chief of the Bureau of Ships. "He called to remind me on that occasion," said James, "that he was not the submarine builder, he was simply the nuclear-plant producer." James said that it was the only time in his four-year tenure as Chief of BuShips that Rickover "was thoroughly dishonest." James continued: "Rickover went to great extremes to disassociate any likelihood of failure of the nuclear plant from the *Thresher* incident. I considered this thoroughly dishonest."

At the court of inquiry that looked into the *Thresher* disaster, Rickover said, "There is no reason to believe any radiological problems were caused by the loss of the *Thresher*." He also told the court that ocean-floor samples from the area showed the bottom to be free of radioactivity. Rickover continued his testimony on a classified basis, behind closed doors. An officer in the room said of Rickover's testimony: "I was damn impressed by his intellectual honesty. When the chips were really down, when lives were at stake, he acted intellectually humble. He said things like, 'I never thought of that' or 'I don't know' or 'Let me go back and talk to my people about that.'"

Rickover's testimony was not made public. However, his views of the *Thresher* disaster can be gleaned from his subsequent appearances before the Joint Committee on Atomic Energy. He said that "the known facts are so meager it is almost impossible to tell what was happening aboard *Thresher*." Then, after admitting the need to look for "further improvements," he launched into a series of criticisms against the frequent rotation of officers, particularly those who were concerned with the *Thresher*'s overhaul; the lack of adequate welding techniques; the poor management and quality control in submarine construction; and the manner in which the Navy's leadership made decisions about submarine requirements.

Significantly, the day after the disaster, Rickover called the first of several meetings to determine means of a faster reactor startup, as it became evident that the initial "minor difficulty" was an emergency reactor scram, or shutdown. The lengthy procedure for restarting the reactor had left the *Thresher* without propulsive power at a critical moment.

In May 1968, the U.S. nuclear-propelled submarine *Scorpion* was lost with all ninety-nine men on board. She was returning to the United States from operations in the Mediterranean; she failed to arrive at Norfolk as scheduled. For several months the Navy searched her predicted track, finally identifying her shattered hull off the Azores in water ten thousand feet deep. There was no communication from the *Scorpion* just before her loss, and her remains could not definitely establish the cause of her loss.

While several theories were put forward based on the limited evidence available—a torpedo explosion, battery explosion, and propeller failure being the most probable—in no way was her reactor plant involved in the casualty.[21]

Indeed, as the U.S. Navy's nuclear submarines steamed through the ocean depths, they established an excellent safety record. True, there were problems with the "boats": the occasional fire, the small *Tullibee* losing her (single) propeller while running submerged in the Mediterranean, and even some relatively minor leakages of radioactive water. But the design of the reactor plants and the training of the submarine crews were sound, thanks largely to Rickover.

Rickover sought to select and train every officer in the submarine force and those in surface nuclear ships who worked in the engineering departments. He undertook this effort by virtue of his "hat" with the AEC. As head of the AEC's Naval Reactors Branch, he could dictate the policies and procedures for personnel that would operate shipboard reactors. And, of course, he dictated that commanding officers of all submarines (and later all surface ships) had to be nuclear-qualified.

His selection process called for his staff to review personnel records, and then for him to personally interview candidates for his program, be they midshipmen from the Naval Academy or Naval Reserve Office Training Corps (NROTC), or lieutenants or higher ranks from the fleet. His interviews were infamous. Was there really a chair in front of his desk with the front legs shorter than the back ones, so that the candidate felt he was slipping? Did he really send men to the broom closet to rethink an answer?

The admiral believed that he could tell in such sessions—which lasted from a couple of minutes to an hour or so—whether or not a man was suitable to be trained to operate his reactors. During these interviews, Rickover would ask questions about the man's studies and grades (although the candidate's records already gave that information), his interests, goals, social life, whether or not he liked animals, and so on.

If the answers didn't please Rickover, he would rant and rave. Candidates were sent to a small room—the "broom closet"—to rethink an answer. The three- or four-star admiral would yell, scream, and even walk out on the hapless midshipman or junior officer. As reports of these sessions reached senior Navy officials and questions were asked about the interviews, another NRB officer was unobtrusively present for the interviews.

At times, a candidate left the interview sure that his career in the Navy was finished, only to find a message waiting for him at his office or back on his ship from the Bureau of Naval Personnel that he was being ordered into the nuclear program. Others, who wanted desperately to enter the Nuclear Navy, found that they had flunked the interview. A few even tried to flunk the interview, having no desire to serve in the program.

But the Rickover scheme did produce an outstanding cadre of officers who manned the Navy's nuclear submarines, the engineering departments of surface ships, and, in time, the nation's civilian nuclear power industry.

●◆●◆✕◆●

Little more than a decade after the loss of the *Scorpion*, there was another "event" involving nuclear energy, and although no lives were lost, the event had more of an impact on the United States. On March 27, 1979, eleven miles from Harrisburg, the capital of Pennsylvania, Unit 2 of the Three Mile Island nuclear power plant, known as TMI-2, was operating normally under fully automatic control. As the overnight shift took over at 11 P.M., the plant was performing perfectly. Operators Craig Faust and Ed Frederick, under shift supervisor Bill Zewe, prepared for a long night in the control room. Faust and Frederick, like Zewe, were former Navy reactor operators who had been through the Rickover-directed nuclear power courses.

At four o'clock the next morning, TMI-2 failed, releasing radioactivity that endangered workers and citizens in the community. The heart of the crisis was a gas bubble that had built up in the core of the new reactor in TMI-2.

Admiral Rickover dispatched specialists from his offices in Pittsburgh and Schenectady, along with the Knolls Atomic Power Laboratory's emergency action coordinating team, to investigate. The critical question was, "Would the bubble explode?" The Rickover experts determined it would not.

The nation was not so sure, and Americans were mesmerized by news of local school children and pregnant women evacuating the area within five miles of the plant on orders of Pennsylvania's governor. They were told that low levels of radioactive gas were in the environment, and they understood that the initial efforts to halt the releases were not successful. Rickover's words on the potential of nuclear accidents came back to haunt: "There are a lot of things that can go wrong and it requires eternal vigilance. All we have to have is one good accident in the United States and it might set the whole game back for a generation."

Rickover's involvement in Three Mile Island during the acute crisis days (which had eased off by March 4, as the bubble was reduced) was not public knowledge, and when he testified before a congressional subcommittee two months after the accident, he was silent on his behind-the-scenes actions. His unusual modesty was not that surprising. For years Rickover had kept the controversial and hazardous side of nuclear power as far from him and his operations as he could. His concern about safety issues and public perception sometimes resulted in his taking convoluted positions. For example, he worried that an accident aboard one of his nuclear submarines would destroy public confidence. So he prohibited their appearance in many foreign and U.S. ports. After the USS *Nautilus* made her historic North Pole transit in 1958, she was ordered into New York City by the White House, but never again would a nuclear ship enter that port nor those of many other major American cities.

There was a notable exception in 1962 when Speaker of the House John W. McCormack wanted the new, nuclear-propelled aircraft carrier *Enterprise* to visit his hometown of Boston on the Fourth of July. Navy brass decided to ignore the Rickover dictum and simply notified him that the *Enterprise* was going to Boston. The decision triggered a dispute between Rickover, several other admirals, and the Secretary of the Navy. The *Enterprise* did go to Boston.

By the late 1970s, Rickover's position on nuclear safety had evolved into one of great complexity. He issued regular warnings, while offering statistics showing there was nothing to fear. He wanted to keep nuclear-propelled ships away from major cities, but he was silent about electric-power reactors near cities. He insisted on training for every man who worked on his reactors, but he did not make the same demands of civilian industry, nor did he offer his training facilities to civilians.

In July 1979, when he was called upon to testify before the president's Commission on the Accident at Three Mile Island, he was relatively moderate; his criticism was oblique rather than direct. In 1975, speaking about his insistence on keeping NRB people at Shippingport, he had said, "I do not think you can depend on self-inspection alone any more than you can depend on every individual to properly report his income tax if there was no one checking up on him. I do not think that is in accord with human nature." In 1979 he reiterated his recommendation that a government representative be kept in nuclear power plants, but he did not say it with the vigor he had used before.

His testimony at the time, before a congressional committee, was similarly muted. Sounding not at all like his former self, he said that "it would be presumptuous on my part to make judgments on such a highly complex subject when I do not have the facts." This from a man who never hesitated to speak out about anything. As for not having the facts, he had access to all the information that the NRB's teams had obtained and produced in their work at Three Mile Island. And he obviously could get whatever other information he wanted.

After Three Mile Island, Rickover began pondering the future of the nuclear world. Behind his crusty exterior, he was increasingly concerned about human beings. President Jimmy Carter quoted him as saying, "I wish that nuclear power had never been discovered."

Rickover, the aggressive technocrat, was struggling over nuclear power. The signs around reactors said, "Danger: Radiation Hazard," and he knew what those signs meant. "I am not a proponent of nuclear power or of any other energy source," he said in a speech in 1979. "All alternatives have their own limitations; none are without risk." Knowing those risks, he tried to find some ground on which he could make his stand. His ground narrowed to this: "The decision whether we should have nuclear power is a political one."

There is a document available that suggests Rickover had deep fears about nuclear power. The document, dated July 18, 1986, is a notarized statement by Jane Rickover, who was then his daughter-in-law. She said Rickover had told her that President Carter had commissioned a full report of the Three Mile Island accident. If the report were published in its entirety, he told her, it "would have destroyed the civilian nuclear power industry because the accident at Three Mile Island was infinitely more dangerous than ever made public." Rickover told her, according to her statement, that "he had used his enormous personal influence with President Carter to persuade him to publish the report only in a highly 'diluted' form." Later, she swore, Rickover "told me that he had come to deeply regret his action in persuading President Carter to suppress the most alarming aspects of that report."

Rickover once set down his "principles for doing your job." One of them was: "It is not easy to admit that what you thought was correct did not turn out that way."

8

Rickover the Man

Commander Edward L. "Ned" Beach was one of the backstage operators in the campaign to promote Rickover in 1951. He later served as naval aide to President Eisenhower, and then commanded the nuclear-propelled submarine *Triton* on her historic underwater voyage around the world in 1960. Certainly, Beach was no foe of Rickover. But, in 1977, while describing the admiral, he called him a man adept at flattering the Congress or the press, yet

> unusually susceptible to the most elementary flattery himself. A man self-serving to an unbelievable degree, devoid of appreciation of or sympathy for the differences in people, intent only on getting his job done as he and he alone conceives it should be done.

What Beach said was true: Rickover's life was his work. But there was a part of him that was not merely work. He once read aloud to an interviewer part of a letter he had written to Ruth Masters Rickover: "Forgive me for not writing more, I am so tired. Above all though, there is the clear thought of you and of my love. Your vision is ever fresh, smiling and lovely. Your likeness and alertness contrasts with my drowsiness. Good night. I shall fall asleep with thoughts of you as my lullaby."

She once wrote of a summer's day in 1953. Her husband had been promoted to rear admiral, and momentarily peace had come into their lives after months of turmoil. She was sitting in the tiny garden she had created behind the Washington apartment house they lived in. She was "watching a hummingbird buzzing ecstatically among the white and pink hollyhocks. The zinnias were coming along splendidly and there would soon be many tomatoes for the salad bowl." Then "a most indignant young man" appeared on the scene. "You've just got to come upstairs, Mother, and tend to that phone. It's ringing and ringing and I have to do my Morse Code practice. I just can't be bothered with all those characters crying for Daddy." She continued, "I sighed and got up, thinking how completely our life had become enslaved to those pesky nuclear reactors. They'd elbowed their way into the family and become its most important members. . . ."

Such a glimpse into the private life of Hyman Rickover—called George by his wife—is extremely rare. Even rarer is an insight into how Ruth Rickover fit into that life, and rarer still is any mention of their son, Robert Masters Rickover, who was then thirteen.

Her sketch of that interrupted summer's day appears in *Pepper, Rice, and Elephants*, a book that was begun in 1954 but was not published until 1975, three years after her death. The book describes the travels of the Rickovers through Southeast Asia in the late 1930s. The book is far more than a travelogue. It is the work of a woman who is indomitable ("became thoroughly blasé about cobras"). Throughout her travels she kept shorthand notes that she then worked into a diary. She took out the diary in the summer of 1953, "checked facts and added bits of history," and began writing. Except for doing research for her husband and offering sharply critical suggestions to him about his writings, she had done little of her own work for several years.[22]

After Robert's birth at Washington's Georgetown University Hospital on October 11, 1940, she became a housewife and mother. But her interest in international law continued, and she would remain what she had been when Rickover first met her— an intellectual steeped in the European tradition of scholarship. Around the time that Robert entered his teens and was attending nearby Alice Deal Junior High School, the Rickovers thought about moving so that their son could have a room of his own. But, when a second apartment became available in their building, they decided to rent that and move Robert into it. So the family lived somewhat separated lives, mother and father in their apartment and son on another floor in the eight-story apartment house.

Ruth Rickover did not live the life of an admiral's wife. There were no white-glove receptions, no calling cards for receptions on the Washington military-political social circuit. The Rickovers were not part of the flag officers' community. If this bothered her, she did not complain. She had her studies, and she had her writing. When Robert was five, she was working for the Carnegie Endowment for International Peace, which in 1945 published her *Handbook of International Organizations in the Americas*.

The Rickovers' apartment house at 4801 Connecticut Avenue stood among many lining the upper reaches of the broad avenue, a major traffic artery that runs from the heart of downtown Washington, through Washington's affluent Northwest quadrant, and crosses the District line into Chevy Chase, Maryland. Residents of those old and stately apartment houses traditionally have been called "cliff dwellers" because most of them have lived in the buildings for decades. Little about the neighborhood has changed since before World War II.

The Rickovers certainly qualified as cliff dwellers. They moved into 4801 around the time that Rickover was assigned to BuShips on the eve of World War II, and they never moved away. Their apartment was large and spartanly furnished. There were no rugs because, Rickover told visitors, he had an allergy to wool. He may have been joking, for he also had an allergy to spending money on what he deemed to be nonessential. Most of the rooms were full of bookshelves for Rickover's ever-growing collection on a variety of subjects, from history and biography to science and technology, and for Ruth's books, in several languages, on international law and European cultural history.

Rickover periodically invited workers from the Naval Reactors Branch to cocktails and dinner. Ever since a drinking episode as a young officer (when he sounded off to a senior officer), Rickover rarely, if ever, drank. But he served liquor, and guests remembered him as a courteous host, quick with compliments to the ladies and eager for conversation on virtually any subject. He kept shoptalk to a minimum, but tensions of the office day did not magically dissipate in the evening at 4801. It was still dinner at the boss's place.

The admiral had long since ceased considering himself a Jew; he told people he was an Episcopalian. After he married Ruth Masters, Rickover left the religion of his birth in a formal, straightforward way by writing a letter about his decision to his parents in Chicago. He lived for years without their forgiveness. Eventually, however, the hurt eased, and Rickover frequently visited his parents in Chicago; they did not visit his home.

In his congressional testimony, he often made allusions to Jesus, although he also cited the Talmud occasionally. That he was Jewish by birth was well known, and charges of anti-Semitism often arose during his promotion fights. While one was going on, Admiral Arleigh Burke, the Chief of Naval Operations, was startled to be told that three rabbis were waiting in his outer office. He asked that they be shown in, but immediately warned them that he could spare little time to hear entreaties about Rickover. "But all they wanted to tell me was that in their opinion he was not Jewish," Burke remembered.

The most efficient way for Rickover to get from 4801 Connecticut Avenue to work was by car—as a passenger, not a driver. And that was how Rickover traveled. He belonged to a carpool, but he was the only member without a car. Men in that ever-changing carpool could recall, decades later, how they were exploited in the service of Rickover's decision to be efficient. He used the time in the car as work time, quizzing driver and fellow passengers on projects, rifling through his inevitable file of "pinks," and, finding something wrong, shouting at the perpetrator if he was in the car.

He was usually compassionate when personal tragedies struck people who worked for him, and his compassion went beyond NRB. When the *Thresher* and the *Scorpion* were lost, official letters of condolences were typed (sometimes with misspellings) and sent out to "the next of kin." Rickover wrote, in his own hand, letters to the widows of married men and the parents of unmarried men. Unlike the impersonal, official letters, the unexpected, handwritten Rickover letters became mementos that the survivors cherished for their compassion.

But his compassion for those who mourned did not usually extend to those who merely wanted time with their families. Time and again he would arrange schedules so that he and his workers traveled on weekends and that no time was wasted during normal workdays. Submarine officers ruefully joked that the designation of nuclear-propelled attack submarines—SSN—meant "Saturdays, Sundays, and Nights." They knew that the nuclear navy did not want "builders of nests and hatchers of eggs." Questions about a prospective candidate's family life appeared frequently in Rickover's notorious interviews.

Unmarried men were asked if they intended to marry; married men were asked whether they had or intended to have children. In the early nuclear days, when candidates were coming from the fleet for nuclear submarine training, a lieutenant commander who had commanded a non-nuclear submarine appeared for the Rickover interview. As the officer recounted the session later, Rickover quickly asked, "How many children do you have?"

"Four," the officer replied.

"What do you do when you come home from your ship?"

"Well, knowing my wife has had a pretty full day, I usually help her with dinner, do the dishes, clean up, and put the kids to bed."

"Oh. You're another one of these goddamn nesters."

The lieutenant commander was unable to respond. He

swallowed his anger, and the interview continued. He was accepted—with the proviso that he spend at least forty hours a week, in addition to his regular duties, preparing for nuclear-power school. He would have no time for nesting.

Vice Admiral William R. Smedberg, a former Chief of Naval Personnel, recalled in his memoirs, "I used to have his Polaris captains come to me and, almost with tears in their eyes, say, 'I can't take it any longer. I can't take it. I've been in command . . . for six consecutive years and I just can't take the pressure of being a commanding officer that much longer. I can't do it, and he [Rickover] wants me now to take out a new Polaris boat.'"

At an age when other couples were settling into retirement, Ruth Rickover was the wife of a man who still worked a seven-day week. In January 1972, she was examined at the Naval Hospital in Bethesda, Maryland, a few miles north of Washington. She was diagnosed as suffering from atherosclerotic heart disease. On May 25, she collapsed after a heart attack at home and was taken to the Bethesda hospital, where she died that night. She was sixty-nine years old. On the night she died, Rickover burned the beautiful letters that she had written to him.

At about 5 A.M. on Thursday, November 16, 1972, a plane carrying Admiral Rickover from New London, Connecticut, landed at Washington's National Airport. Rickover had spent a long, taxing Wednesday at the Electric Boat yard, where the hostility toward him and his methods was steadily mounting. He walked rapidly away from the plane toward his office in the Crystal City complex, about a mile from the airport.

A mile's walk would not ordinarily strain him, but he was even frailer than usual. Coworkers had noticed his decline since his wife's death; he had withdrawn even more within himself, and a man who had known and observed

Rickover for years realized for the first time that he had never had any close friends.

Soon after having walked the mile to his office, he collapsed, striking his head as he fell. Unconscious and bleeding from a head wound, he was given emergency treatment and then taken to Bethesda Naval Hospital. At first the Navy said he was suffering from exhaustion. But a few days later, the hospital announced that he had suffered "a minor heart attack," was in the coronary-care unit, and would be kept under treatment for a few weeks.

Rickover was well-known in the hospital, one of the few Navy institutions he had never publicly criticized. Doctors, nurses, medical corpsmen, and his own NRB staff were ready for what would happen next: Rickover's suite would be transformed into an office, and he would insist on people bringing work to him, including, of course, the pinks.

The working-hospitalization tradition had begun in 1946, when, up from Oak Ridge for a hernia operation, he had labored from his bed. Rickover had similarly set up shop in Bethesda after a heart attack in July 1961. He soon recovered, and he became such a model of recovery that in 1964 the American Heart Association presented him with its Heart-of-the-Year Award for having "inspired people everywhere with new hope."

During his hospitalization in 1972, the "official" twelve-hour days continued. He did not slow down; and seven months later, he was back in Bethesda, this time for what the Navy described as treatment for a respiratory ailment.

On January 19, 1974, Rickover married Navy Commander Eleonore Ann Bednowicz, a Navy nurse who was forty-three years old. Rickover had met her during his 1972 stay at Bethesda. She later was transferred to the Naval Training Center at Great Lakes, Illinois. When she and Rickover were married, their wedding plans were so secret that her superiors at the training center were not aware that she was going on leave to get married. The Naval Reactors Branch found out when, without explanation, Rickover gruffly ordered double accommodations for a forthcoming trip to London. NRB workers, accustomed to carrying out orders with a minimum of questions, could only assume that Rickover had a traveling companion in mind, but they did not ask for an identity.

The wedding was at St. Celestine's Roman Catholic Church in Elmwood Park, a Chicago suburb. They were married by the Reverend John Powell, a Jesuit from Loyola University. News of the wedding was revealed after it took place. Commander Rickover, bright and personable, retired from the Navy the following November. She became interested in the hospice movement and joined the board of directors of the Hospice of Northern Virginia.

<hr>

The Navy marked the twenty-fifth anniversary of the commissioning of the *Nautilus* on September 30, 1979, with a celebration at the Washington Navy Yard. Rickover was praised as a genius whose "dogged pursuit of excellence have [*sic*] had a profound effect on the entire Navy." Rickover was not at the celebration; he had not even responded to his invitation.

Rickover no longer lived at 4801 Connecticut, and the Naval Reactors Branch was no longer on Constitution Avenue, hidden within the massive complex of "temporary" wooden buildings erected on the Washington Mall during World War I. Now, he and Eleonore lived near his work, for his apartment and the NRB were in the same complex of Virginia concrete known as Crystal City. Every morning, just before eight, a Navy car picked him up and took him around the block from his home, in the Buchanan House, to the building that housed NRB, National Center No. 2. From their balcony at the rear of Buchanan House, his wife could wave to him as he entered the office building.

In mid-1981, the Rickovers moved to The Representative, an expensive, five-year-old condominium a mile from Crystal City on Arlington Ridge Road. His personal life changed with his marriage to Eleonore Bednowicz, for she was more outgoing than Ruth, and the Rickovers attended more parties and dinners.

The Navy had also changed; there were many nuclear ships. The Navy's leadership had also changed, with "nucs" in many senior positions. But Rickover himself was largely unchanged. He was still fighting battles. Perhaps he was winning fewer, or perhaps he was simply fighting fewer.

9

Getting Rid of Rickover

On July 2, 1951, a Navy selection board met in Arlington Annex, an ugly, tan-colored building on a ridge overlooking the Pentagon and, across the Potomac River, the Capitol. The selection board, consisting of nine admirals, would select eligible captains for promotion to the rank of rear admiral. In addition to selecting line officers, the board would select a small number of restricted line officers—engineering duty officers (EDO) among them. The board members met in secret. No minutes were kept of their deliberations and no one was to discuss the details of their voting. When the board's selections were announced, there were two EDOs on the promotion list—Rickover was not one of them.

Rickover reacted by deciding that he would no longer rely on the Navy promotion system. He already had a degree of independence because of his connection with the Atomic Energy Commission, and through his connections in Congress, which in the future would make him "Admiral of the Hill." But by turning his back on the Navy, Rickover began a long and bitter struggle that would continue until 1982, when the U.S. Navy finally got rid of

Hyman G. Rickover.

On Flag Day 1952, an overhead crane lifted a steel plate of the *Nautilus* and placed it on a building way at the Electric Boat yard. President Truman officiated at the ceremony. Speaking after the president, Gordon Dean, Chairman of the Atomic Energy Commission made a brief statement, in which he said, "There are many people who have played a role in the events which have led to this ceremony, but if one were to be singled out for special notice, such an honor should go to Captain H. G. Rickover, whose talents we share with the Bureau of Ships and whose energy, drive, and technical competence have played such a large part in making this project possible."

After the speeches, President Truman spotted Rickover sitting in a car and walked over to shake his hand. The president's train of uniformed, beribboned naval officers looked on in horror as Rickover remained seated in the car. News of the incident soon began making the rounds of the Pentagon. Rickover, it was said, was embarrassing the Navy. But there were officers who pointed to the calendar and said that the Navy would not have to put up with Rickover much longer.

About this time, Clay Blair, Jr., a World War II submariner who wrote for *Time* and *Life* magazines, received a telephone call at his home from Ray Dick, who had been with Rickover since the earliest days at Oak Ridge. Blair had written a glowing article about Rickover after he had been passed over for a promotion in 1951. As Blair recalled the phone call, Dick said it was vital that they "meet privately on a matter of utmost urgency about the nuclear-submarine program." Dick, with a touch of the dramatic, suggested that they meet within the hour at a large rock on Beach Drive in Rock Creek Park, a meandering, path-laced woodland that runs through the middle of Washington.

For hours, Dick talked while Blair listened. Dick said that Rickover was in trouble—and so was America's nuclear-submarine program. A Navy selection board was to convene shortly, and if Rickover was again passed over, not only would the Navy lose an outstanding officer, but the United States would lose years in the race to get nuclear submarines before the Soviet Union. Dick unburdened himself about the sufferings of Rickover: the anti-Semitism, the snubs by senior officers, the conspiracy not merely to deny him promotion but, much more important, to break up his team. He warned: "If Rickover goes, the project is going to die."

On July 8, 1952, the selection board met and again passed on Rickover; this meant that within one year, Captain Rickover, by law, would have to leave the Navy. But several members of Congress wanted to keep him in the Navy. Among those who started lobbying to retain Rickover were then-Representative Henry M. Jackson of the Joint Committee on Atomic Energy and Representative Sidney Yates, from Rickover's hometown of Chicago. Yates cited anti-Semitism in the Navy as the reason Rickover was not promoted. Yates, who would serve in the House until 1999, said that his defense of Rickover was among the moments in his public life of which he was most proud. Eleanor Roosevelt even sent him a handwritten note congratulating him on his courage.

Blair wrote an article for *Time* with the headline "Brazen Prejudice," and, although the prejudice referred to was Navy line officers' prejudice against specialists like EDOs, people in and out of the Navy read it as a signal that something more was involved. (There was no mention in the Blair story that Rickover was Jewish; by this time he considered himself an Episcopalian.)

NRB staffers attempted to have nuclear contractors raise the promotion issue to their congressional delegations. Attempts were also made to reach President Eisenhower. One of Rickover's assistants, Commander E. E. Kintner, had his brother-in-law raise the subject with John Eisenhower, the son of the president. Kintner's brother-in-law had introduced John and Barbara Eisenhower and was a good friend. The attempts to keep Rickover in the Navy seemed numberless, and Rickover—directly or indirectly—used all of them.

Finally, the Navy capitulated. Another selection board was

convened and at the direction of the Secretary of the Navy it considered engineering captains who were specialized in nuclear propulsion. Captain H. G. Rickover was belatedly selected for promotion to rear admiral.

Blair topped off his one-man public relations campaign by writing a book-length tribute to Rickover—*The Atomic Submarine and Admiral Rickover*, published in 1954. "The book was written almost exclusively in Rickover's office," Blair recalled to the authors. "They gave me an office and a typewriter, and I had total access to all but classified information." In advertisements about the book, the publisher said, "WARNING! The Navy will not like this book." (Later, in reading lists that he prepared of the NRB staff and nuclear trainees, Rickover listed the book as *Admiral Rickover and the Atomic Submarine*.)

Rickover had broken all the rules, and yet here was Rickover—Rear Admiral Rickover, now—suddenly one of the most well-known officers in the Navy. The ultimate proof of this came on January 11, 1954, when he made the cover of *Time* magazine.

The Navy was reeling. A tradition and selection procedures had been publicly disregarded for one man. Congress had brazenly waded into the Navy's private promotion system. Rickover supporters had swarmed to Capitol Hill like lobbyists. Nothing like this had happened before. Never had a captain made a spectacle out of being passed over; never had a single officer so openly used Congress for his personal purposes.

<hr/>

Rickover was promoted to vice admiral in 1958 without much notice. With each passing year, he was becoming vulnerable again because of a seemingly immutable law—Title X, U.S. Code—that said an officer had to retire when he or she became sixty-four years old, and for Rickover that time would come in January 1964.

Rickover began his new campaign for retention in March

1962, when he met with members of the Joint Committee on Atomic Energy aboard the aircraft carrier *Enterprise.* "As long as I am able and both I and others feel I can do a useful job," he told the lawmakers, "I would like to stay on." The Navy did not want him to stay on. Senior officers had passed that word to the White House by President John F. Kennedy's naval aide. Kennedy briefly considered making Rickover Commissioner of Education, because of the admiral's continual interest in improving American schools, but that idea faded quickly. Secretary of the Navy Fred Korth developed a compromise solution: retire Rickover, but keep him on as a civilian, working for the Atomic Energy Commission as director of the Navy's reactor program. Negotiations with Rickover began. The issue was tabled after the assassination of President Kennedy and the replacement of Korth by Paul H. Nitze by President Lyndon B. Johnson.

During his almost four years as Secretary of the Navy, Nitze would have several run-ins with Rickover. For example, the Navy's leadership wanted to employ gas turbine engines to propel surface warships. These were aircraft-type jet engines that, in surface ships, provided the advantages of low weight-to-power ratios, easy maintenance, and smaller size than steam plants. But Rickover would have none of it. He feared that the adoption of gas turbines in U.S. warships—they were already being used in Soviet and British ships—would delay or even halt the use of nuclear propulsion in surface ships.

Learning that Rickover was to testify about surface ship propulsion before a congressional committee, Nitze summoned him to his office and asked if he understood the Navy's position on the matter. Rickover said no.

Working with his staff, Nitze formally developed the Navy's position on gas turbines for surface ships. That weekend, he personally wrote out that position, making it succinct and easily understandable. He gave it to Rickover. He asked if Rickover understood the Navy's position, and Rickover responded in the affirmative.

The next day, Rickover testified before the committee, saying that he did not understand the Navy's position. He then began a lengthy dissertation on the value of surface ship nuclear propulsion. The U.S. Navy was delayed several years in adopting that efficient propulsion system, which now drives all of the U.S. Navy's cruisers, destroyers, and frigates.

———◆◆◆◆———

At the request of the Secretary of Defense, Nitze took up the task of dismissing Rickover and produced a solution: after Rickover retired in January 1964, Nitze would recall him to active duty for two years, with the possibility of another extension after that. Rickover accepted the two-year solution, but it appeared that there would not be a second two-year extension. In mid-1967, Nitze was about to become Deputy Secretary of Defense to Robert S. McNamara, who believed that Rickover should go. McNamara told Nitze to take that decision to President Johnson. The president agreed and told Nitze to see the Joint Committee on Atomic Energy "and tell them I'm all for this . . . if you can get their backing, I'm all for it."

Nitze passed the president's sentiments on to Senator John O. Pastore of Rhode Island, chairman of the Joint Committee, on which he had served almost continuously since 1952. As Nitze recalled, Pastore said, "I've got to talk to other members of my committee. Call me in three or four days."

Nitze dutifully returned to Capitol Hill. As he entered Pastore's inner office, Nitze found assembled there Senators Clinton P. Anderson of New Mexico and Henry M. Jackson of Washington, as well as Representative Chet Holifield of California. All were long-serving members of the Joint Committee; Holifield had been a member when it was established in 1947. There was one other man in the room—Rickover. "I understand that you are trying to get me fired," Rickover said to Nitze in a matter-of-fact tone.

"I was flabbergasted," Nitze later related. Here he had the approval of the Secretary of Defense and the president to dismiss an officer, an action that was both legal and proper. Then Jackson, in a short speech about Rickover, said, "Everybody agrees that at some time Rickover might be relieved—but that time has not come yet."

Thus began a ritual in Rickover's life. Every two years the Joint Committee on Atomic Energy would remind the Atomic Energy Commission and the U.S. Navy that Rickover was indispensable and should be kept on duty, and every two years the Secretary of the Navy would comply. The ritual would continue until 1981, when President Ronald Reagan took office—the thirteenth president under whom Rickover had served, if you count President Woodrow Wilson, when Midshipman Rickover entered the U.S. Naval Academy.

◆◆×◆◆

On January 25, 1981, five days after President Reagan's inauguration, the 6,900-ton, 360-foot-long nuclear attack submarine *Jacksonville* went down the Thames River, into Long Island Sound, and out into the Atlantic Ocean on her initial sea trials. Rickover stood in the maneuvering compartment of the submarine's engineering spaces. In accordance with the established test program, one of the maneuvers the submarine would go through was known as the "quick stop" or "crashback," when the engines would be put on full astern.

There were 136 Navy men on board, plus fifty civilian technicians and engineers, among them thirty-five from the Electric Boat yard in Groton, Connecticut, where the *Jacksonville* had been built. During the quick stop, which would come at the end of a full-power submerged run, the submarine was in a dangerous position. If she developed "sternway," by picking up significant astern speed, the submarine could go out of control, plunge in a steep dive, and possibly exceed her collapse depth. Recovery would depend on how fast the order was given to speed ahead.

Rickover was giving the orders on the *Jacksonville* trials, as he had done during nuclear submarine trials since the *Nautilus* submerged in those waters almost exactly twenty-six years before. Now, standing in the maneuvering room on the upper level of the *Jacksonville*'s engineering spaces, in the after section of the submarine, he delayed a full minute in giving the ahead-speed order. This delay caused the submarine to develop an astern speed of over nine knots. The submarine began tilting and going deeper.

Once full control was regained, Rickover ordered the quick-stop maneuver repeated. This time, the Navy officers on board devised a way to outwit Rickover by giving him false information about the relative speed of the ship. But Rickover's delays in orders still caused astern speeds, though not as great as the first time. He ordered the maneuver four more times, and each time the sternway exceeded three knots.

Vice Admiral E. B. Fowler—head of Navy shipbuilding and, although lower in rank, Rickover's nominal boss—was aboard the *Jacksonville*. A few days after the trials, Electric Boat officials advised Fowler that they had "grave concern" about the quick-stop incident. An EB memo on the incident rapidly circulated through the Navy's shipbuilding and nuclear reactor commands. "It was the type of thing that everybody makes a Xerox copy of," said a man who had seen the original report of the incident.

The report went into the Reagan White House's "Rickover file." Some of the documents referred to Rickover's war against Electric Boat, the country's largest builder of submarines and a major division of the General Dynamics Corporation, the nation's largest defense contractor. There were also Rickover tirades against P. Takis Veliotis, who had run the Electric Boat yard since 1977.

By the beginning of 1981, EB was building twenty nuclear attack submarines, plus several of the billion-dollar Trident strategic missile submarines. In July, the nuclear attack submarine *La Jolla* went to sea on trials. When Rickover was directing the quick-stop maneuver, again officers on board conspired to deceive Rickover to prevent the submarine from going astern. Rickover's orders still came late and the *La Jolla* developed sternway—this time exceeding eleven knots. As a result, the submarine took a nosedive at an angle of more than forty degrees and went down 240 feet before the crew regained full control.

Veliotis wrote to the Chief of Naval Operations, Admiral

Thomas B. Hayward, about the way Rickover had handled the *Jacksonville* and *La Jolla* trials. Copies soon appeared at the White House and on the desks of several newspaper editors. Navy leaders closed ranks on the incident. Hayward said the maneuver "is challenging to a crew with respect to maintaining the submarine at a nearly neutral trim angle and within its ordered depth band, but I would not categorize it as hazardous."

In August 1981, Secretary of the Navy John F. Lehman, Jr., speaking at the National Press Club, attacked EB for having "injected a new and very disruptive element into our business relations," as he discussed a new multimillion-dollar claim made by the company against the Navy. He also criticized their use of "platoons of corporate lawyers"—a phrase that seemed to be right out of Rickover's testament. During the subsequent question-and-answer session, Lehman praised Rickover and left the impression he would be extended on active duty the following January.

General Dynamics chairman David Lewis raced to the White House, clutching a copy of Lehman's speech. He was ushered in to see presidential counselor Edwin Meese III, who only then seemed to have realized the full significance of the Rickover issue. (As former president Jimmy Carter later told a television interviewer, "the defense contractors were out to get Rickover for a long time. He was an embarrassment to them.") The White House staff accelerated its soundings of key members of Congress and a strategy began to develop to get rid of Rickover. The Navy's Rickover file—consisting almost entirely of his commendations and awards and little else—was perused, and meetings were held with Secretary of Defense Caspar Weinberger; Secretary Lehman; Meese's deputy, Robert Garrick, a reserve rear admiral; and others who knew "the Rickover story," including a few, select members of Congress. A key member involved with nuclear issues responded to Garrick's question about how he would oppose Rickover's dismissal with the brief comment, "I will write a letter of protest to the White House." The comment reflected the views of several key senators and representatives.

Admiral Rickover was to speak at the commissioning ceremonies for the first Trident submarine, the *Ohio,* at Electric

Boat on Veterans Day, November 11. The *Ohio* was the largest undersea craft yet built in the United States—a submarine five feet longer than the Washington Monument is tall. Rickover made a typical speech that inventoried the size of the nuclear navy. Secretary Lehman spoke of Tridents and grand strategy but did not mention Rickover. Vice President George H. W. Bush spoke Rickover's name as he reeled off the names of those on the platform, but he had nothing to say about the man in his speech. The final speaker, Admiral Hayward, did not mention Rickover's name. The omission was significant.

Two days later, in the office of Secretary of Defense Weinberger, Rickover was told that he was being retired, but that President Reagan wanted him to be an adviser on nuclear power. Rickover refused. (As Rickover told it later, he already knew because his wife had called him and said, "It's on the radio that you're fired.")

On January 8, 1982, President Reagan invited Rickover to the White House for a traditional rite: the departing official is honored by handshake and a few moments of valuable presidential face time. With Weinberger and Lehman present, Rickover used the occasion to berate the president, telling him that he was "in the pocket of industry" and that he "does not understand what is going on." Weinberger and Lehman—whom Rickover called a "pissant [who] knows nothing about the Navy"—were astonished. The session ended abruptly.[23]

Later that month, Rickover appeared before a sparsely attended session of the Joint Committee on Atomic Energy. In the last time he would appear before a committee as an official of the government, he spoke for nearly three hours in his raspy voice, complaining about, among other things, claims lawyers, midshipmen who play too much football, corporate executives, the Defense Department civilians, the Justice Department prosecutors who don't prosecute . . . .

But then came something so odd that people who had listened to Rickover for decades could not agree whether he spoke as a prophet too-long ignored or as an angry old man left bitterly out in the cold: "Take the number of nuclear submarines. . . .

What's the difference if we have 100 or 200? . . . I think we probably will destroy ourselves . . . so what difference will it make? Some new species will come up that might be wiser than we are. . . ."

Congress gave Rickover a parting gift: a declaration that the Navy should give him an office in the Washington Navy Yard so he could continue as an adviser on nuclear issues. Few people asked him for any advice. Much of his time was devoted to the Admiral H. G. Rickover Foundation, dedicated to examining technological, commercial, and educational issues relating to energy. He was particularly interested in the Rickover Summer Science Institute, attended by high school students who were high achievers in science and mathematics. (In 1986 he abruptly withdrew from the foundation, which then became the Center for Excellence in Education.)

Tributes came to him in retirement. Congress awarded him a second Congressional Gold Medal. The Naval Academy he so despised named an engineering building after him. A new attack submarine, through the efforts of Secretary Lehman, was named the *Hyman G. Rickover*. She was launched at EB on August 27, 1983.[24] Mrs. Eleonore Rickover christened the submarine. The honor of christening a nuclear-propelled submarine had been denied Ruth Masters Rickover, who had seen the snub as one of the ways used by the "stupid windbags" who run the Navy to "really hurt my husband."

At the luncheon following the launching, Rickover reminded his audience that all had gone well at EB until General Dynamics took over and the manager had "attempted to impose his will on the United States Navy." That manager, Veliotis, was not in attendance. He had fled to Greece after being charged with fraud over irregularities in defense contracts.

In July 1985, Rickover suffered a slight stroke. He recovered but, weakened, he developed pneumonia, had a second stroke, and remained in declining health. On July 8, 1986, he died in his home in Arlington, Virginia. He was buried in Arlington National Cemetery. Inscribed on his gravestone are the words *63 years active duty* and *Father of the Nuclear Navy.*

1. Rickover's school records show that he was born in Makow on August 24, 1898; his official Navy biography says he was born on January 27, 1900. Throughout his official life, he recorded his birth year as 1900.
2. Abraham would work at his trade—except for a brief attempt at retirement at age seventy-six—until he died in 1960 at the age of eighty-five. His wife Rachel, as she became known in America, died in 1968.
3. The Bureau of Navigation controlled naval personnel until May 13, 1942, when it was changed to the Bureau of Naval Personnel.
4. The Dutch Navy had developed the snorkel to permit Dutch submarines in the East Indies to operate submerged to escape the heat.
5. A smaller, coastal version of this design, the Type XXIII, was also developed; a few of those boats undertook combat patrols during the war.
6. The AEC was disbanded in 1974, with its functions transferred mainly to the Energy Research and Development Administration (subsequently the Department of Energy) and the Nuclear Regulatory Commission.
7. BTU stands for British thermal unit. The report, "Proposed Submarine Powered by Nuclear Transformations," dated November 19, 1945, is appended to Minutes of Submarine Officers Conference, November 6, 1945 (Report of November 14, 1945).
8. GUPPY stood for Greater Underwater Propulsive Power, with the letter "y" added for phonetic purposes.
9. In 1955, the Submarine Thermal Reactor was redesignated S1W for the land prototype and S2W for the *Nautilus* plant.
10. Title VIII of the Department of Defense Authorization Act for Fiscal Year 1975.

11.   In 1975, the Navy's DLG/DLGN-type "frigates" were reclassified as cruisers to better reflect their size and role.

12.   Named for Soviet physicist Pavel Alekseevich Cherenkov.

13.   Beach had been President Eisenhower's naval aide and had previously commanded a diesel-electric submarine.

14.   The *Triton*'s conning tower (within her fairwater) permitted the submarine's pressure hull to be kept isolated from the atmosphere during the transfer. The heavy cruiser *Macon* had been in Argentine waters in conjunction with President Eisenhower's visit to that country.

15.   Initially, although additional funds were provided to the Navy for SLBM development, by 1959 the Navy was forced to cancel development of the Regulus II land-attack cruise missile and the P6M Seamaster flying-boat bomber, and delay construction of an aircraft carrier to help pay for the Polaris project. At the time, all three of these programs were viewed by the Navy as strategic strike weapons.

16.   David A. Rosenberg, "Admiral Arleigh Burke," in Robert William Love, Jr., *The Chiefs of Naval Operations*. Annapolis, Md.: Naval Institute Press, 1980, 277. Admiral Burke served an unprecedented six years as CNO, from 1955 to 1961.

17.   Lt. Millard A. Cosby, USNR, "Polaris—Deep Deterrent," unpublished paper [n.d.], p. 7. A Polaris warhead weight of 600 pounds (compared to a Jupiter warhead of 1,600 pounds with a similar explosive yield) is cited in Richard G. Hewlett and Francis Duncan, *Nuclear Navy, 1946-1962*. Chicago: University of Chicago Press, 1974, 309.

18.   Hewlett and Duncan, *Nuclear Navy*, 308.

19.   Ibid, 309.

20.   This remains history's worst submarine disaster. See Norman Polmar, *Death of the USS Thresher*. New York: Lyons Press, 2001.

21.   See Stephen Johnson, *Silent Steel: The Mysterious Death of the Nuclear Attack Sub USS* Scorpion. Hoboken, N.J.: John Wiley & Sons, 2006.

22.   See Ruth Masters Rickover, *Pepper, Rice, and Elephants*. Annapolis, Md.: Naval Institute Press, 1975.

23.   See John F. Lehman, Jr., *Command of the Seas: Building the 600 Ship Navy*. New York: Charles Scribner's Sons, 1988.

24.   There are reports that Lehman pushed the naming of a submarine for Rickover to avoid congressional action to name an aircraft carrier for the admiral.

This foreshortened biography of Admiral Rickover relies on three general sources that the authors used for their comprehensive *Admiral Rickover: Controversy and Genius* (New York: Simon & Schuster, 1982). First, the words of Admiral Rickover that he spoke before congressional committees—more than one million of them—supported by thousands of pages of prepared statements and supplementary papers. Second, interviews with, and oral histories made by, scores of individuals who knew and worked with (and in some instances against) Rickover—naval officers, enlisted men and women, and civilians involved with nuclear submarines, education, shipbuilding, and the electric power industry, the Department of Defense, and other parts of American society. And, third, the hundreds of reports and letters concerning Admiral Rickover and his various activities that reside in the Navy's Operational Archives and the National Archives, in libraries, and in the collections of the Naval Academy, Navy Department, National Education Association, Department of Energy, and the private collections of several individuals.

Ships' logs (held by the National Archives) and magazine and newspaper articles were also used.

These sources have been supplemented by more recently published material and additional interviews for this volume.

Several books on Admiral Rickover and nuclear submarines are considered to be "must" reading for those who seek to understand the controversy and genius of Admiral Rickover. Among the most professionally prepared was the official

Department of Energy history by Richard G. Hewlett and Francis Duncan, *Nuclear Navy, 1946–1962* (Chicago: University of Chicago Press, 1974).

The first book about Rickover was Clay Blair, Jr.'s, *The Atomic Submarine and Admiral Rickover* (New York: Henry Holt, 1954). "The book was written almost exclusively in Rickover's office," he told the authors of this book. "They gave me an office and a typewriter, and I had total access to all but classified information." Mrs. Rickover (Ruth Masters), a scholar and fine stylist, read the manuscript—and said that she did not like it; she apparently held toward Blair the special disdain that scholars often have for journalists.

Rickover, said Blair, "seemed to like the book. He bought lots of copies."

Three other books were written with Rickover's encouragement and assistance. Francis Duncan wrote *Rickover and the Nuclear Navy: The Discipline of Technology* (Annapolis, Md.: Naval Institute Press, 1990) and *Rickover: The Struggle for Excellence* (Annapolis, Md.: Naval Institute Press, 2001). Duncan, a professional historian, worked for Admiral Rickover from 1969 to 1987. Less of a professional history and more a book of reminiscences, interspersed with numerous factual errors, is Theodore Rockwell's *The Rickover Effect: How One Man Made a Difference* (Annapolis, Md.: Naval Institute Press, 1992).

A rare personal view of Rickover will be found in Ruth Masters Rickover's, *Pepper, Rice, and Elephants* (Annapolis, Md.: Naval Institute Press, 1975). The book, published after Ruth Masters passed away, was edited and prepared for publication by Rickover. Four books by officers who commanded nuclear submarines provide unique insight of those undersea craft and of Admiral Rickover: Captain William R. Anderson, USN, *Nautilus 90 North* (Cleveland, Ohio: World Publishing, 1959); Captain Edward L. Beach, USN, *Around the World Submerged* (New York: Holt, Rinehart, Winston, 1962); Commander James Calvert, USN, *Surface at the Pole* (New York: McGraw-Hill, 1960); and

Commander George P. Steele, USN, *Seadragon: Northwest Under the Ice* (New York: E. P. Dutton, 1962).

Several books that describe the development and operation of nuclear submarines as well as describing the Navy during critical periods for nuclear propulsion are recommended to the reader: Norman Friedman, *U.S. Submarines Since 1945: An Illustrated Design History* (Annapolis, Md.: Naval Institute Press, 1994); John F. Lehman, Jr., *Command of the Seas: Building the 600 Ship Navy* (New York: Charles Scribner's Sons, 1988); Norman Polmar, *Atomic Submarines* (Princeton, N.J.: D. Van Nostrand, 1963), and *Death of the Thresher* (Philadelphia, Pa.: Chilton Books, 1964; revised edition *Death of the USS Thresher*, New York: Lyons Press, 2001); Norman Polmar and Kenneth J. Moore, *Cold War Submarines: U.S. and Soviet Submarine Design and Construction* (Washington, D.C.: Brassey's, 2003); Patrick Tyler, *Running Critical: The Silent War, Rickover, and General Dynamics* (New York: Harper & Row, 1986); Gary E. Weir, *Forged in War: The Naval-Industrial Complex and American Submarine Construction, 1940–1961* (Washington, D.C.: Naval Historical Center, 1993); and Admiral Elmo R. Zumwalt, Jr., USN, *On Watch* (New York: Quadrangle, The New York Times Book Co., 1976).

Admiral Zumwalt was Chief of Naval Operations during the critical period 1970–1974; John Lehman was Secretary of the Navy from 1981 to 1987, and was a key figure in the "firing" of Admiral Rickover.

In addition to the above books, two magazines have contained numerous articles related to Admiral Rickover and to nuclear submarines—the U.S. Naval Institute *Proceedings* (monthly) and *The Submarine Review* (quarterly).

Anderson, Capt. William R., USN. *Nautilus 90 North*. Cleveland, Ohio: World Publishing, 1959.

Beach, Capt. Edward L., USN. *Around the World Submerged*. New York: Holt, Rinehart, Winston, 1962.

Blair, Clay. *The Atomic Submarine and Admiral Rickover*. New York: Holt, Rinehart, Winston, 1954.

Calvert, Comdr. James, USN. *Surface at the Pole*. New York: McGraw-Hill, 1960.

Duncan, Francis. *Rickover: The Struggle for Excellence*. Annapolis, Md.: Naval Institute Press, 2001.

————. *Rickover and the Nuclear Navy: The Discipline of Technology*. Annapolis, Md.: Naval Institute Press, 1990.

Friedman, Norman. *U.S. Submarines since 1945: An Illustrated Design History*. Annapolis, Md.: Naval Institute Press, 1994.

Groves, Maj. Gen. Leslie R., USA. *Now It Can Be Told*. New York: Harper and Brothers, 1962.

Hewlett, Richard G., and Francis Duncan. *Nuclear Navy, 1946–1962*. Chicago: University of Chicago Press, 1974.

Johnson, Stephen. *Silent Steel: The Mysterious Death of the Nuclear Attack Sub USS Scorpion*. Hoboken, N.J.: John Wiley & Sons, 2006.

Lehman, John F., Jr., *Command of the Seas: Building the 600 Ship Navy*. New York: Charles Scribner's Sons, 1988.

Polmar, Norman. *Atomic Submarines*. Princeton, N.J.: D. Van Nostrand, 1963.

————. *Death of the Thresher*. Philadelphia, Pa.: Chilton Books,

1964; revised edition *Death of the USS Thresher*. New York: Lyons Press, 2001.

_____, and Thomas B. Allen. *Rickover: Controversy and Genius.* New York: Random House, 1982.

_____, and Kenneth J. Moore. *Cold War Submarines: U.S. and Soviet Submarine Design and Construction*. Washington, D.C.: Brassey's, 2003.

Rickover, Ruth Masters. *Pepper, Rice, and Elephants*. Annapolis, Md.: Naval Institute Press, 1975.

Steele, Comdr. George P., USN. *Seadragon: Northwest Under the Ice.* New York: E. P. Dutton, 1962.

Tyler, Patrick. *Running Critical: The Silent War, Rickover, and General Dynamics*. New York: Harper & Row, 1986.

Weir, Gary E. *Forged in War: The Naval-Industrial Complex and American Submarine Construction, 1940-1961*. Washington, D.C.: Naval Historical Center, 1993.

Zumwalt, Adm. Elmo R., Jr., USN. *On Watch*. New York: Quadrangle, The New York Times Book Co., 1976.

Index

THOMAS B. ALLEN's writings range from articles for *National Geographic Magazine* to books on military subjects. He is the coauthor, with Norman Polmar, of *Spy Book: The Encyclopedia of Espionage*, which *Time* magazine called "the definitive spy-vs.-spy" book. He and Polmar also wrote *World War II: America at War 1941-1945*, which the *Library Journal* gave its "highly recommended" rating, and said the "accurate and enjoyable" entries "encourage compulsive browsing." The book was selected by the New York Public Library as one of the reference books of the year. Their *Merchants of Treason*, an analysis of post-Rosenberg espionage by Americans, received critical acclaim. Tom Clancy said on the book's jacket, "This book should be required reading for every security officer in the United States."

Allen and Polmar are also the authors of *Code-name: Downfall*, subtitled *The Secret Plan to Invade Japan and Why Truman Dropped the Bomb*; *Rickover: Controversy and Genius*; and *Ship of Gold*, a novel of sex, spies, and gold. With F. Clifton Berry they were coauthors of the CNN-Turner Publishing book *War in the Gulf*, published in June 1991. Mr. Polmar also was editor of this book.

Mr. Allen is the writer and coproducer of *Offerings at the Wall*, a book on the objects and notes left at the Vietnam Veterans Memorial. His *Possessed*, a study of a modern-day exorcism, has been cited by the *Washington Post*: "with the aid of a hot discovery—an eyewitness diary of the exorcism . . . Allen has written an impressively sober and fair-minded book." Mr. Allen coauthored, with Paul Dickinson, *The Bonus Army: An American Epic*. For *National Geographic* he has written *The Blue and the Gray*, *Vanishing Wildlife of North America*, *George Washington*, *Spymaster*, *Remember Pearl Harbor*, and *Harriet Tubman, Secret Agent*.

In January 1992, Doubleday published *Murder in the Senate*, a novel written by Mr. Allen and William Cohen, former Senator and Secretary of Defense. The *Washington Post* said the book "straddles the line between mystery and political-conspiracy thriller and works well on both levels."

Mr. Allen has written or coauthored more than thirty books. He is a former senior book editor for National Geographic Society, and before that was managing editor of Chilton Books. Both he and Mr. Polmar appear regularly on television as subject experts.

NORMAN POLMAR is an analyst, consultant, and author specializing in naval, aviation, and intelligence issues. In 1997–1998 he held the Ramsey Chair of aviation history at the National Air and Space Museum in Washington, D.C.

Since 1980 Mr. Polmar has been a consultant to several senior officials in the Navy and Department of Defense, and has directed several studies for U.S. and foreign shipbuilding and aerospace firms. From 1982 to 1986, and since December 2002 he has been a member of the Secretary of the Navy's Research Advisory Committee (NRAC). He was also a consultant to the Director of the Los Alamos National Laboratory. Mr. Polmar has served as a consultant to three U.S. Senators and two members of the House of Representatives, and as a consultant or adviser to three Secretaries of the Navy and two Chiefs of Naval Operations.

Prior to 1980, Mr. Polmar was an executive and before that an analyst with research firms specializing in strategic, submarine, and naval issues. In addition to conducting studies and analyses for U.S. government agencies and for the aerospace and shipbuilding industries, he has consulted to the navies of Australia, China, and Israel.

Mr. Polmar has written or coauthored more than forty books and numerous articles on strategic, aviation, and naval subjects. Seven previous books were coauthored with Thomas B. Allen. Among his recent books are the two-volume *Aircraft Carriers: A History of Carrier Aviation and its Influence on World Events* and *Cold War Submarines: U.S. and Soviet Submarine Design and Construction*, the latter written in collaboration Mr. Kenneth J. Moore, an American submarine technologist, and with the Russian submarine design bureaus Rubin and Malachite.

He was associate producer and coauthor with John D. Gresham, formerly chief researcher for Tom Clancy, of the Discovery Channel film *DEFCON-2*, which starred Tom Clancy. Subsequently, he and Gresham authored the book *DEFCON-2: Standing on the Brink of Nuclear War During the Cuban Missile Crisis*; Tom Clancy wrote the foreword for the book.

He is the longtime author of the reference books *Ships and Aircraft of the U.S. Fleet* and *Guide to the Soviet Navy*, which were published at three-year intervals by the U.S. Naval Institute. These books are recognized internationally as the leading references in their fields.

Messrs. Allen and Polmar are both residents of the Washington, D.C. area.

MILITARY PROFILES
AVAILABLE

Cushing: Civil War SEAL
Robert J. Schneller

Doolittle: Aerospace Visionary
Dik Alan Daso

Eisenhower: Soldier-Statesman of the American Century
Douglas Kinnard

Farragut: America's First Admiral
Robert J. Schneller

Foch: Supreme Allied Commander of the Great War
Michael S. Neiberg

Haig: The Evolution of a Commander
Andrew Wiest

Hindenburg: Icon of German Militarism
William J. Astore and Dennis Showalter

Semmes: Rebel Raider
John M. Taylor